BEST POP SONGS

FOR EASY GUITAR

ISBN 978-1-4950-0069-0

HAL•LEONARD®
CORPORATION
7777 W. BLUEMOUND RD. P.O. BOX 13819 MILWAUKEE, WI 53213

Visit Hal Leonard Online at
www.halleonard.com

STRUM AND PICK PATTERNS

This chart contains the suggested strum and pick patterns that are referred to by number at the beginning of each song in this book. The symbols ⊓ and ⌄ in the strum patterns refer to down and up strokes, respectively. The letters in the pick patterns indicate which right-hand fingers play which strings.

p = thumb
i = index finger
m = middle finger
a = ring finger

For example; Pick Pattern 2
is played: thumb - index - middle - ring

You can use the 3/4 Strum and Pick Patterns in songs written in compound meter (6/8, 9/8, 12/8, etc.).
For example, you can accompany a song in 6/8 by playing the 3/4 pattern twice in each measure.
The 4/4 Strum and Pick Patterns can be used for songs written in cut time (¢) by doubling the note time values in the patterns. Each pattern would therefore last two measures in cut time.

All of Me

Words and Music by John Stephens and Toby Gad

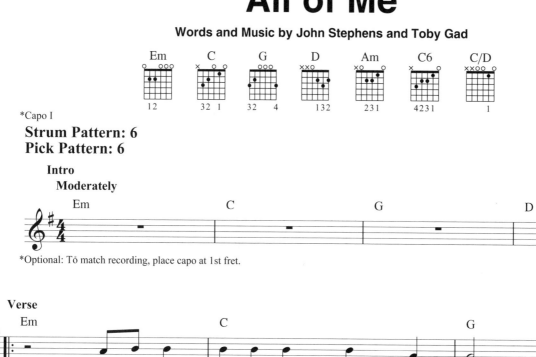

*Capo I

Strum Pattern: 6
Pick Pattern: 6

Intro
Moderately

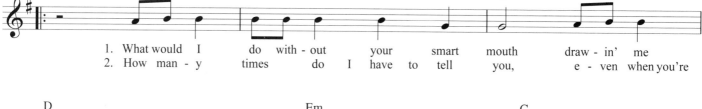

*Optional: To match recording, place capo at 1st fret.

Verse

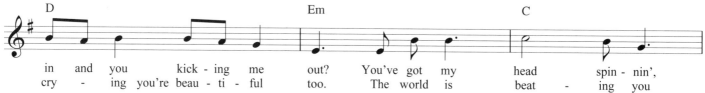

1. What would I do with-out your smart mouth draw-in' me
2. How man-y times do I have to tell you, e-ven when you're

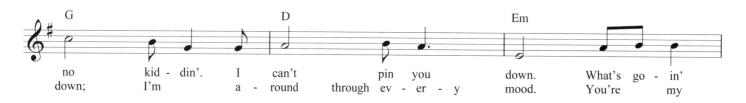

in and you kick-ing me out? You've got my head spin-nin',
cry-ing you're beau-ti-ful too. The world is beat-ing you

no kid-din'. I can't pin you down. What's go-in'
down; I'm a-round through ev-er-y mood. You're my

on in that beau-ti-ful mind? I'm on your mag-i-cal mys-ter-y
down-fall, you're my muse, my worst dis-trac-tion, my rhy-thm and

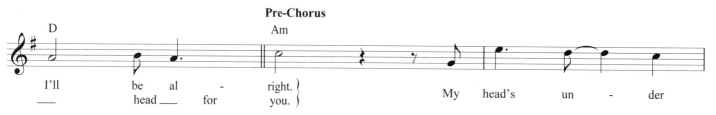

ride, and I'm so diz-zy, don't know what hit me but
blues. I can't stop sing-in', it's ring-in' in my

Pre-Chorus

I'll be al-right.
head for you.

My head's un-der

4

water, _____ but I'm breath - ing fine.

You're cra - zy and I'm out ____ of my mind. 'Cause

𝄋 Chorus

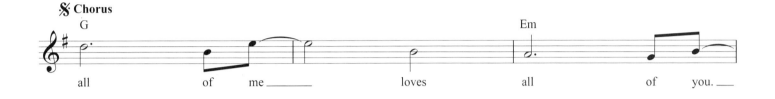

all of me _____ loves all of you. ___

___ Love your curves and all your edg - es, all your

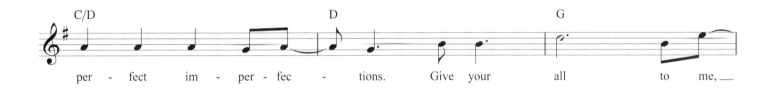

per - fect im - per - fec - tions. Give your all to me, ___

___ I'll give my all to you. _____ You're my

end and my be - gin - ning. E - ven when I lose, I'm win -

- ning 'cause I give you all _____ of me. ___

5

Bad Day

Words and Music by Daniel Powter

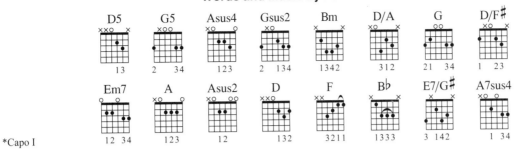

*Capo I

Strum Pattern: 3
Pick Pattern: 3

Intro
Slow

*Optional: To match recording, place capo at 1st fret.

Verse

1. Where is the mo-ment we need-ed the most? ____
2. You stand in the line just to hit a new low. ____

You kick up the leaves and the mag-ic is lost. ____
You're fak-in' a smile with the cof-fee to go. ____

Pre-Chorus

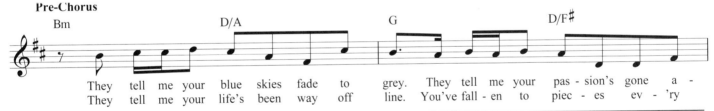

They tell me your blue skies fade to grey. They tell me your pas-sion's gone a-
They tell me your life's been way off line. You've fall-en to piec-es ev-'ry

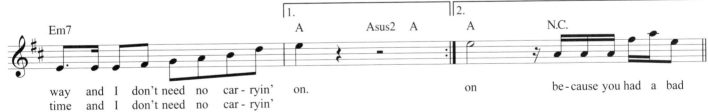

way and I don't need no car-ryin' on. on be-cause you had a bad
time and I don't need no car-ryin'

Chorus

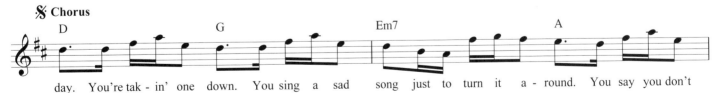

day. You're tak-in' one down. You sing a sad song just to turn it a-round. You say you don't

know. You tell me don't lie. You work at a smile and you go for a ride. You had a bad

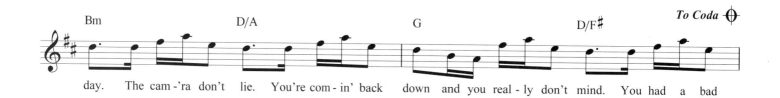

day. The cam-'ra don't lie. You're com-in' back down and you real-ly don't mind. You had a bad

Piano Solo

day. _____ You had a bad day.

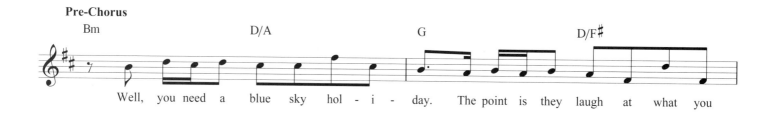

Pre-Chorus

Well, you need a blue sky hol - i - day. The point is they laugh at what you

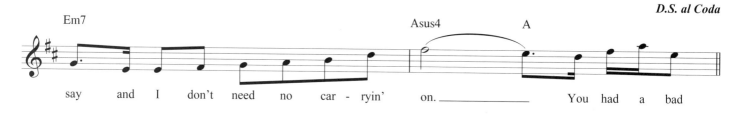

D.S. al Coda

say and I don't need no car-ryin' on. _____ You had a bad

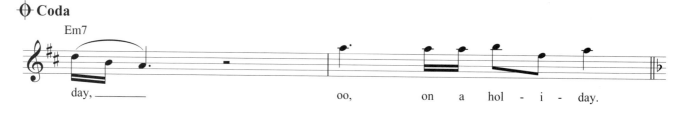

Coda

day, _____ oo, on a hol - i - day.

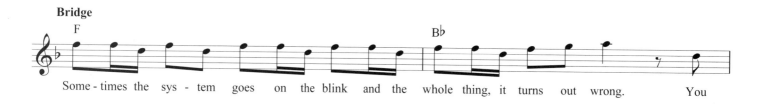

Bridge

Some - times the sys - tem goes on the blink and the whole thing, it turns out wrong. You

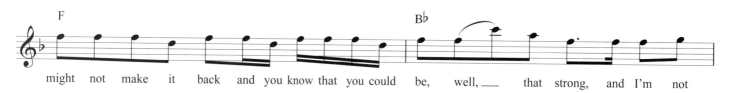

might not make it back and you know that you could be, well, ___ that strong, and I'm not

wrong, _____ yeah, _____ yeah. _____

Verse

3. So where is the pas - sion when you need it the most? ___ Oh, you and

I. You kick up the leaves and the mag - ic is lost ___ 'cause you had a bad

*Let chord ring.

Outro-Chorus

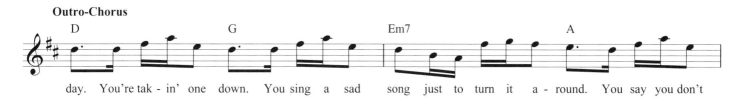

day. You're tak - in' one down. You sing a sad song just to turn it a - round. You say you don't

know. You tell me don't lie. You work at a smile and you go for a ride. You had a bad

day. You've seen what you like. And how does it feel one more time? You had a bad

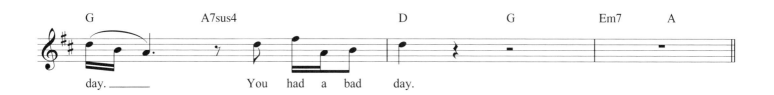

day. _____ You had a bad day.

Repeat and fade

Baby Can I Hold You

Words and Music by Tracy Chapman

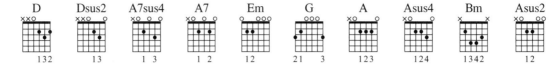

Strum Pattern: 3
Pick Pattern: 3

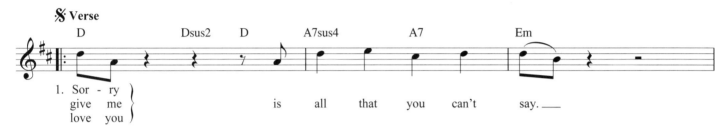

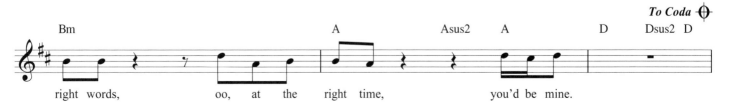

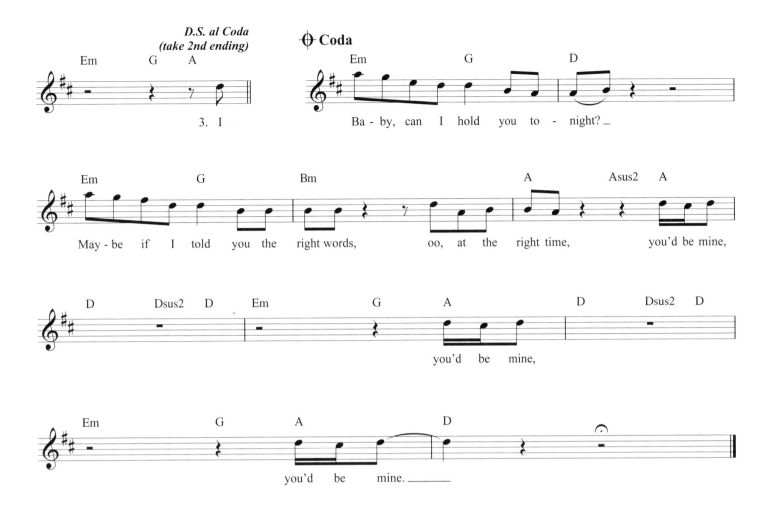

D.S. al Coda
(take 2nd ending)

Coda

3. I

Ba - by, can I hold you to - night?

May - be if I told you the right words, oo, at the right time, you'd be mine,

you'd be mine,

you'd be mine.

Black Horse and the Cherry Tree

Words and Music by Katie Tunstall

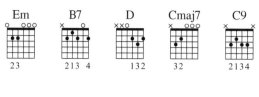

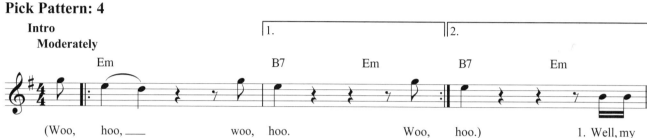

Strum Pattern: 2
Pick Pattern: 4

(Woo, hoo, ___ woo, hoo. Woo, hoo.) 1. Well, my

Verse

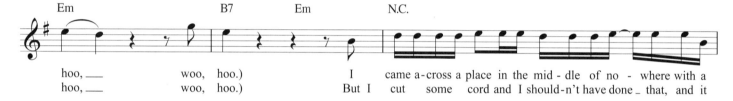

heart knows me bet- ter than I know my- self so I'm gon- na let it do all the talk- in'. (Woo,
heart had a prob- lem in the ear- ly hours, so I stopped it dead for a beat or two. (Woo,

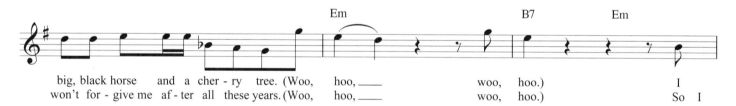

hoo, ___ woo, hoo.) I came a- cross a place in the mid- dle of no - where with a
hoo, ___ woo, hoo.) But I cut some cord and I should- n't have done _ that, and it

big, black horse and a cher- ry tree. (Woo, hoo, ___ woo, hoo.) I
won't for- give me af- ter all these years. (Woo, hoo, ___ woo, hoo.) So I

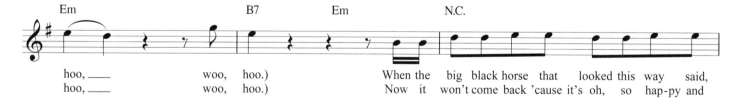

fell in fear up- on ___ my back. I said, "Don't look back, just keep on walk- ing." (Woo,
sent her to a place in the mid- dle of no- where with a big, black horse and a cher- ry tree. (Woo,

hoo, ___ woo, hoo.) When the big black horse that looked this way said,
hoo, ___ woo, hoo.) Now it won't come back 'cause it's oh, so hap- py and

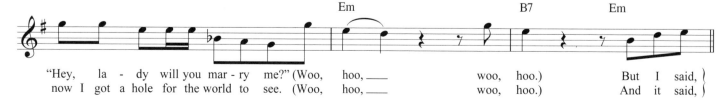

"Hey, la - dy will you mar- ry me?" (Woo, hoo, ___ woo, hoo.) But I said,
now I got a hole for the world to see. (Woo, hoo, ___ woo, hoo.) And it said,

Brave

Words and Music by Sara Bareilles and Jack Antonoff

*Tune down 1 step:
(low to high) D-G-C-F-A-D

Strum Pattern: 5
Pick Pattern: 5

Verse
Moderately slow

1. You can be a-maz-in', you can turn a phrase in-to a wea-pon or a drug.
2. Ev-'ry-bod-y's been there, ev-'ry-bod-y's been stared down by the en-e-my.

*Optional: To match recording, tune down 1 step.
**Sung one octave higher.

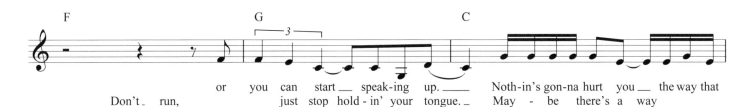

You can be the out-cast or be the back-lash of some-bod-y's lack of love,
Fall-en for the fear and done some dis-ap-pear-in', bow down to the might-y.

Don't run, or you can start speak-ing up. Noth-in's gon-na hurt you the way that
just stop hold-in' your tongue. May-be there's a way

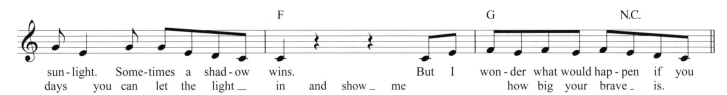

words do when they set-tle 'neath your skin, kept on the in-side and no
out of the cage where you live. May-be one of these

sun-light. Some-times a shad-ow wins. But I won-der what would hap-pen if you
days you can let the light in and show me how big your brave is.

𝄋 Chorus

***C

say } what you wan-na say and let the words fall out hon-est-ly.
(3.) Say }

***3rd time, N.C., next 4 meas.

I wan-na see you be brave with what you wan-na say and let the words fall

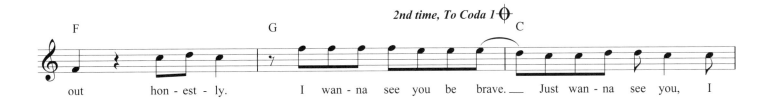

2nd time, To Coda 1 ⊕

F / G / C

out hon - est - ly. I wan - na see you be brave. __ Just wan - na see you, I

F / Am / G

just wan - na see you, __ I just wan - na see you, _____ I wan - na see you be brave. __

3rd time, To Coda 2 ⊕

C / F / Am

__ Just wan - na see you, I just wan - na see you, _____ just wan - na see you, _____

⊕ **Coda 1**

D.C. al Coda 1 **Bridge**

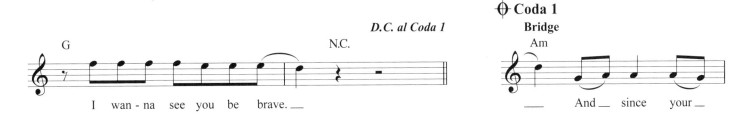

G / N.C. / Am

I wan - na see you be brave. __ ___ And __ since your __

C / C/E F / C/E F

his - to - ry of si - lence won't do you an - y good, did you think it would?

Am / C / Gsus4

Let your words__ be an - y - thing but emp - ty. Why don't you tell them the truth? __

D.S. al Coda 2 ⊕ **Coda 2** **Outro-Chorus**

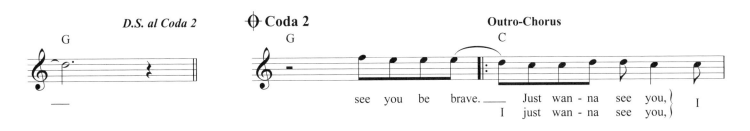

G / G / C

__ see you be brave. __ Just wan - na see you, I
I just wan - na see you, I

1. / 2.

F / Am / G / G

just wan - na see you, I just wan - na see you. _____

Building a Mystery

Words and Music by Sarah McLachlan and Pierre Marchand

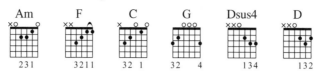

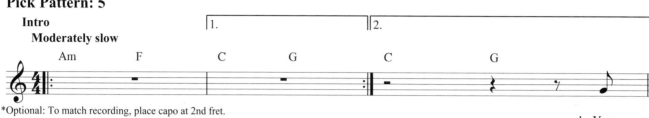

*Capo II

Strum Pattern: 1
Pick Pattern: 5

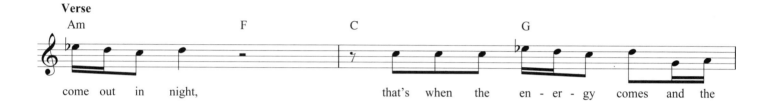

*Optional: To match recording, place capo at 2nd fret.

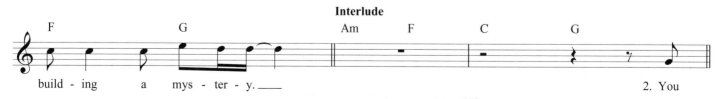

Counting Stars

Words and Music by Ryan Tedder

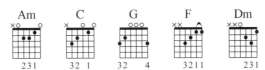

*Capo IV

Strum Pattern: 1
Pick Pattern: 5

Chorus
Moderately

Late-ly I been, I been los-in' sleep   dream-in' a-bout the things that

*Optional: To match recording, place capo at 4th fret.

we could be. But ba-by, I been, I been pray-in' hard.

Said no more count-in' dol-lars, we'll be count-in' stars.   Yeah, we'll be count-in'

Interlude

___ stars. _____

1.   2.
                                1. I   see   this

Verse

life   like a swing-in' vine,_ swing my heart a-cross the line._ In my face is flash-in' signs,
love,   and I feel it burn   down this riv-er, ev-'ry turn._ Hope is a four-let-ter word.

seek it out and ye shall find. }
Make that mon-ey, watch it burn. } Old,   but I'm not that old. Young,   but I'm not that bold. And

I been los - in' sleep dream - in' a - bout the things that we could be. But

ba - by, I been, I been pray - in' hard. Said no more count - in' dol - lars,

3rd time, To Coda ⊕ 1.

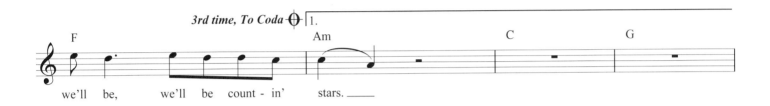

we'll be, we'll be count - in' stars. ____

2.

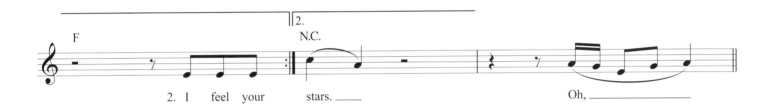

2. I feel your stars. ____ Oh, ____

Bridge

N.C.(Am) *Play 4 times*

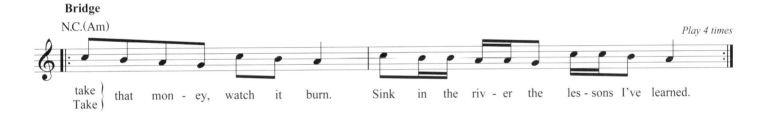

take / Take } that mon - ey, watch it burn. Sink in the riv - er the les - sons I've learned.

D.S. al Coda

Ev - 'ry - thing that kills me makes me feel a -

*Let chords ring.

⊕ **Coda**

Outro

{ stars. / **Take } that mon - ey, watch it burn. Sink in the riv - er the les - sons I've learned. Take that mon - ey, watch it burn.

**Vocals overlap.

1. 2.

Sink in the riv - er the les - sons I've learned. Sink in the riv - er the les - sons I've learned.

Carry On

Words and Music by Jeff Bhasker, Andrew Dost, Jack Antonoff and Nate Ruess

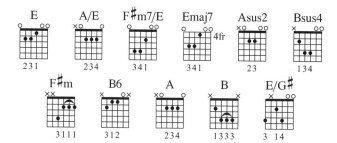

*Capo I

Strum Pattern: 3
Pick Pattern: 3

Intro
Moderately

*Optional: To match recording, place capo at 1st fret.

1. Well, I woke up to the sounds of si - lence, the

cars were cut-ting like knives in a fist fight. And I

found you with a bot-tle of wine, with your head in the cur-tains and heart like the Fourth of Ju - ly.

Pre-Chorus

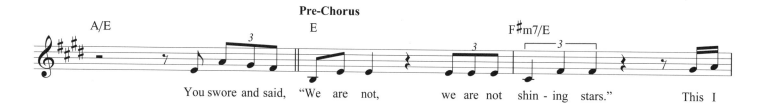

You swore and said, "We are not, we are not shin - ing stars." This I

know; __ I nev - er said we are. Though I've nev - er been through hell like that, I've

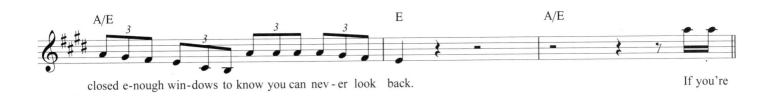

closed e-nough win-dows to know you can nev-er look back. If you're

%Chorus

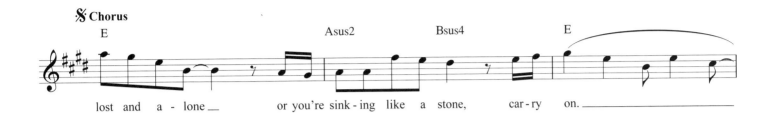

lost and a - lone __ or you're sink-ing like a stone, car-ry on. _____

__ May your past be the sound of your feet up-on the ground, car-ry

2nd time, To Coda 1 ⊕
3rd time, To Coda 2 ⊕

Interlude

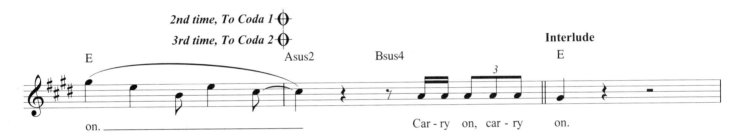

on. _____ Car-ry on, car-ry on.

2. So I

Verse

met up with some friends at the edge of the night at a bar off Sev-en-ty - five.

And we talked and talked a - bout how our par-ents will die, all our neigh -

- bors and wives.   But I   like   to   think   I   can

cheat   it   all,   to make   up   for   the   times   I've   been   cheat - ed   on.   And it's

nice   to   know ____   when I   was   left   for   dead,   I   was   found and now I don't roam these streets.   I   am

D.S. al Coda 1   ⊕ **Coda 1**   **Bridge**

not   the ghost you are   to   me. If you're   ____   Oh, ____   and my

head   is   on   fire,   but my   legs   are   fine.   Af - ter   all,   they   are   mine. _____

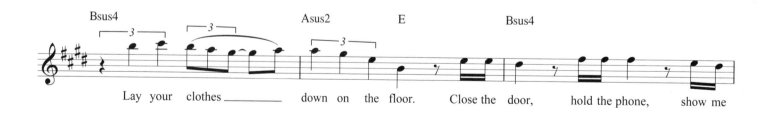

Lay your clothes _____   down   on   the   floor.   Close the door,   hold the phone,   show me

Guitar Solo

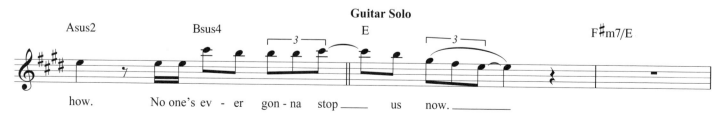

how.   No one's ev - er gon - na stop ____   us   now. _____

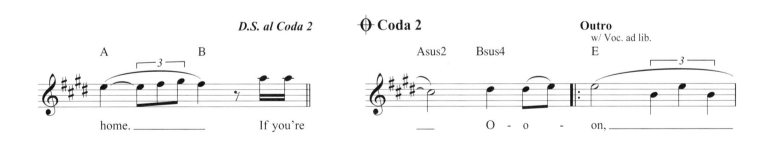

Chasing Cars

Words and Music by Gary Lightbody, Tom Simpson, Paul Wilson, Jonathan Quinn and Nathan Connolly

Strum Pattern: 1
Pick Pattern: 5

26

Come On Get Higher

Words and Music by Matt Nathanson and Mark Weinberg

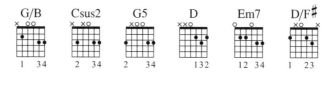

*Capo II

Strum Pattern: 2
Pick Pattern: 1

Intro
Moderately slow

Verse

*Optional: To match recording, place capo at 2nd fret.

1. I miss the sound of your voice, __
2. I miss the sound of your voice, __

and I miss the rush of your skin. __   And I miss the still of the si-
the loud-est thing __ in my head. __   And I ache __ to re-mem-

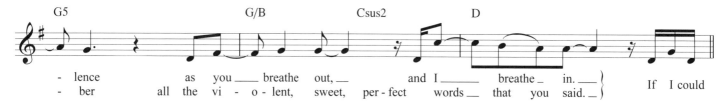

- lence   as you __ breathe out, __   and I _____ breathe __ in. __   If I could
- ber   all the vi - o - lent,   sweet, per - fect   words __ that you said. __   If I could

Pre-Chorus

walk on wa - ter,   if I could tell you what's next, __   I'd make you be - lieve, __   I'd

Chorus

make you for - get. ____   So,   come on, get high - er,   loos - en my   lips.

Faith and de - sire   in the swing of your hips.   Just   pull me down hard ___   and drown __

___ me in love. __   So,   come on, get high - er, loos - en my lips.   Faith and de - sire   in the swing of your hips. Just

Dark Horse

Words and Music by Katy Perry, Jordan Houston, Lukasz Gottwald, Sarah Hudson, Max Martin and Henry Walter

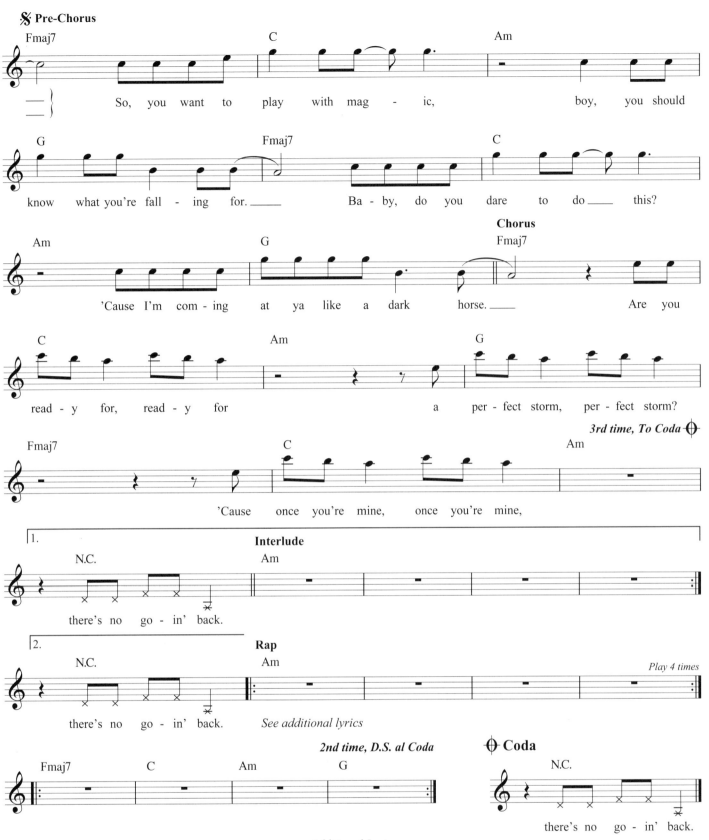

Additional Lyrics

Rap Uh, she's a beast, I call her Karma,
She'll eat your heart out like Jeffrey Dahmer.
Be careful, try not to lead her on.
Shorty heart is on steroids, 'cause her love is so strong.
You may fall in love when you meet her, if you get the chance, you better keep her.
She's sweet as pie, but if you break her heart, she'll turn cold as a freezer.
That fairy tale ending with a knight in shining armor,
She can be my Sleeping Beauty. I'm gon' put her in a coma.
Now I think I love her, Shorty so bad, sprung and I don't care.
She ride me like a roller coaster, turned the bedroom into a fair.
Her love is like a drug, I was try'n' to hit it and quit it,
But lil' mama so dope, I messed around and got addicted.

Daylight

Words and Music by Adam Levine, Max Martin, Sam Martin and Mason Levy

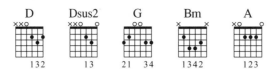

Strum Pattern: 6
Pick Pattern: 6

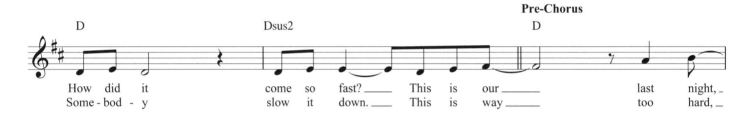

Chorus

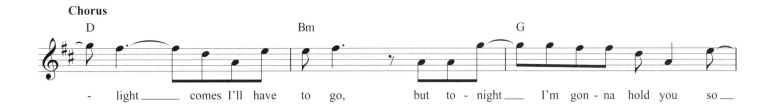

- light _____ comes I'll have to go, but to - night _____ I'm gon - na hold you so _____

_____ close. 'Cause in the day - light _____ we'll be on our own, but to - night _____

_____ I need to hold you so _____ close. Oh. _____ Oh. _____

_____ Oh. _____ Oh. _____

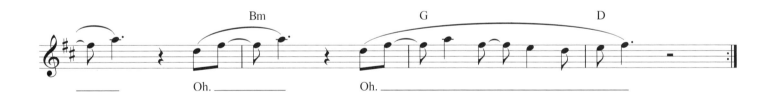

_____ Oh. _____ Oh. _____

Bridge

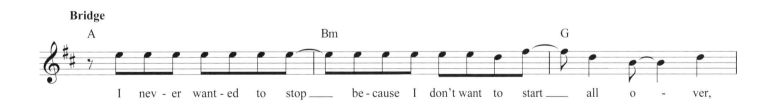

I nev - er want - ed to stop _____ be - cause I don't want to start _____ all o - ver,

start all o - ver. _____ I was a - fraid of the dark, _____ but now it's all that I want, _____

all that ___ I want, all that ___ I want.	And when the day-

*Let chord ring.

Chorus

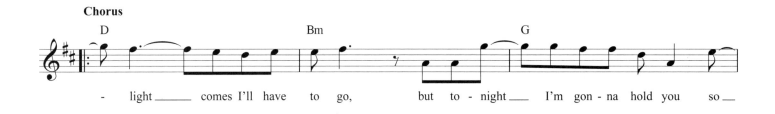

- light _____ comes I'll have to go,	but to - night ___ I'm gon - na hold you	so ___

___ close. 'Cause in the day - light _____ we'll be on	our own,	but to - night ___

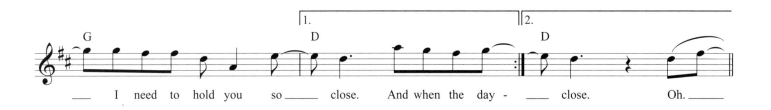

|1.	|2.

___ I need to hold you so _____ close.	And when the day - ___ close.	Oh. ___

_____	Oh. _____	Oh. _____

_____	Oh. _____	Oh. _____	Oh. ____

|1.	|2.

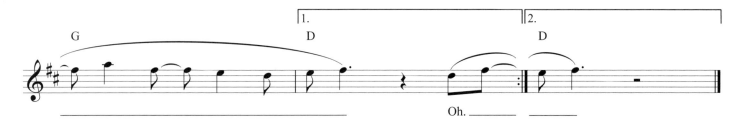

_____	Oh. _____

Get Lucky

Words and Music by Thomas Bangalter, Guy Manuel Homem Christo, Pharrell Williams and Nile Rodgers

Chorus

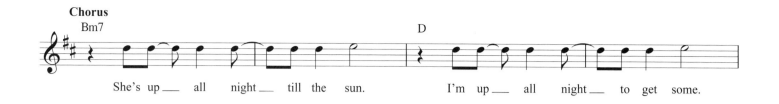

She's up ___ all night ___ till the sun.   I'm up ___ all night ___ to get some.

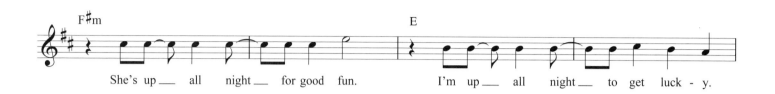

She's up ___ all night ___ for good fun.   I'm up ___ all night ___ to get luck - y.

We're up ___ all night ___ till the sun.   We're up ___ all night ___ to get some.

3rd time, To Coda

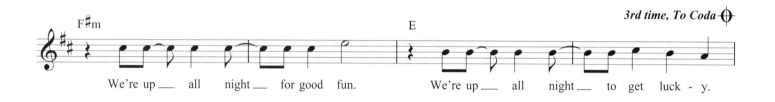

We're up ___ all night ___ for good fun.   We're up ___ all night ___ to get luck - y.

We're up ___ all night ___ to get luck - y.   We're up ___ all night ___ to get luck - y.

1.

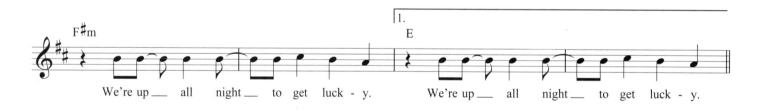

We're up ___ all night ___ to get luck - y.   We're up ___ all night ___ to get luck - y.

Interlude

2.

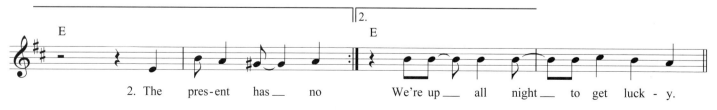

2. The pres-ent has ___ no   We're up ___ all night ___ to get luck - y.

Bridge

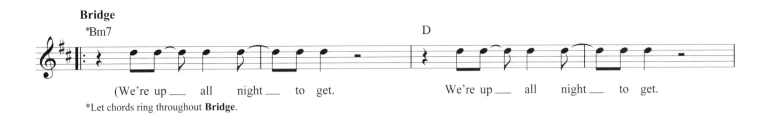

(We're up ___ all night ___ to get. We're up ___ all night ___ to get.

*Let chords ring throughout **Bridge**.

We're up ___ all night ___ to get. We're up ___ all night ___ to get.

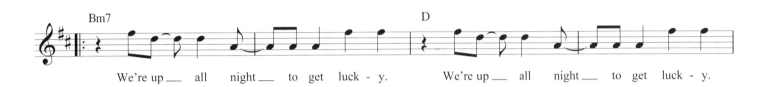

We're up ___ all night ___ to get luck - y. We're up ___ all night ___ to get luck - y.

2nd time, D.S. al Coda

We're up ___ all night ___ to get luck - y. We're up ___ all night ___ to get luck - y.)

Coda

We're up ___ all night ___ to get luck - y. We're up ___ all night ___ to get luck - y.

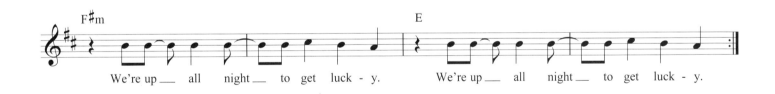

We're up ___ all night ___ to get luck - y. We're up ___ all night ___ to get luck - y.

Outro

Repeat and fade

Flake

Words and Music by Jack Johnson

2nd time, D.S. al Coda

Play 7 times

3. (The)

Outro-Verse

4., 5. *See additional lyrics*

Additional Lyrics

2. I know she loves the sunrise,
   No longer sees it with her sleeping eyes and…
   I know that when she said she's gonna try,
   Well, it might not work because of other ties and…
   I know she usually has some other ties and, ah,
   I wouldn't want to break 'em, nah, I wouldn't want to break 'em.
   Maybe she'll help me to untie this,
   But until then, well, I'm gonna have to lie, too.

4. Ev'rything you know about me now, baby, you gonna have to change,
   You gonna call it by a brand new name, oo, oo, oo.
   Please, please, please don't drag me…
   Please, please, please don't drag me…
   Please, please, please don't drag me down.

5. Just like a tree down by the water, baby, I shall not move,
   Even after all the silly things you do, oo, oo, oo.
   Please, please, please don't drag me…
   Please, please, please don't drag me…
   Please, please, please don't drag me down.

Gone, Gone, Gone

Words and Music by Gregg Wattenberg, Derek Fuhrmann and Todd Clark

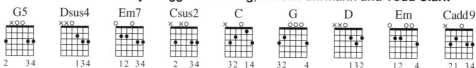

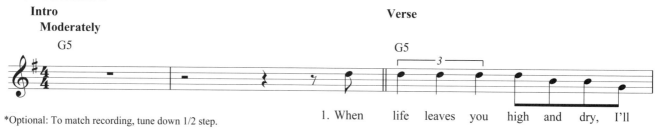

*Tune down 1/2 step:
(low to high) E♭-A♭-D♭-G♭-B♭-E♭

Strum Pattern: 1
Pick Pattern: 5

Intro
Moderately

*Optional: To match recording, tune down 1/2 step.

1. When life leaves you high and dry, I'll

be at your door to-night if you need help, ___ if you need help. ___ I'll

shut down the cit-y lights. I'll lie, cheat, I'll beg and bribe to make you well, ___ to

make you well. ___ When en-e-mies are at your door, I'll carry you a-way ___ from war if
fall like a sta-tue, I'm gon-na be there to catch you, put you

you need help, ___ if you need help. ___ Your hope dang-lin' by a string, I'll
on your feet, ___ you on your feet. ___ And if your well is emp-ty, not a

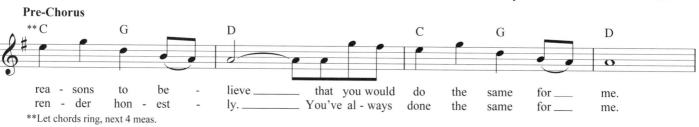

share in your suf-fer-ing to make you well, ___ to make you well. ___ Give me
thing will pre-vent me. Tell me what you need. ___ What do you need? ___ I sur-

Pre-Chorus

rea-sons to be-lieve _____ that you would do the same for ___ me.
ren-der hon-est-ly. _____ You've al-ways done the same for ___ me.

**Let chords ring, next 4 meas.

Chorus

And I would }
So I will } do it for ____ you, ____ for ____ you. ____ Ba - by,

I'm not mov - in' on. I'll love you long af - ter you're gone. For ____ you, ____ for ____

you. ____ You will nev - er sleep a - lone. I'll love you long af - ter you're gone, and

1.

Interlude

2.

long af - ter you're gone, gone, gone.   2. When you   long af - ter you're gone, gone,

Bridge

gone. You're my back - bone, ____ you're my cor - ner - stone. ____ You're my crutch when my

legs stop mov - in'. You're my head start, ____ you're my rug - ged heart. ____

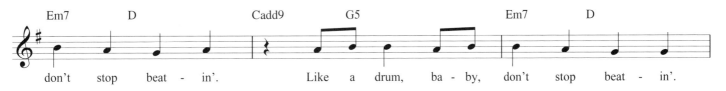

____ You're the pulse that I've al - ways need - ed.   Like a drum, ba - by,

don't stop beat - in'.   Like a drum, ba - by, don't stop beat - in'.

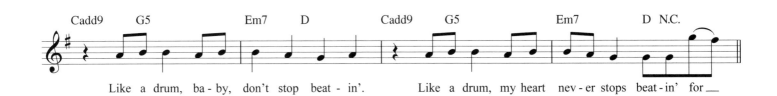

Like a drum, ba - by, don't stop beat - in'. Like a drum, my heart nev - er stops beat-in' for __

Chorus

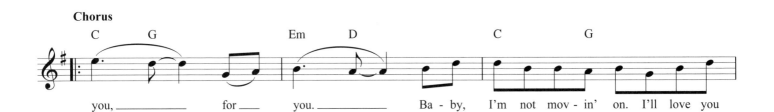

you, _____ for __ you. _____ Ba - by, I'm not mov-in' on. I'll love you

long af - ter you're gone. For __ you, _____ for __ you. _____ You will

nev - er sleep a - lone. I'll love you long af - ter you're gone. For __ long, long __ af - ter you're

Interlude

gone. Like a drum, ba - by, don't stop beat - in'. Like a drum, ba - by, don't stop beat - in'.

Like a drum, ba - by, don't stop beat - in'. Like a drum, my heart

Outro

nev - er stops beat - in' for you. And long af - ter you're gone, gone,

gone, I'll love you long af - ter you're gone, gone, gone.

42

Happy

from DESPICABLE ME 2
Words and Music by Pharrell Williams

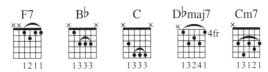

Strum Pattern: 3
Pick Pattern: 3

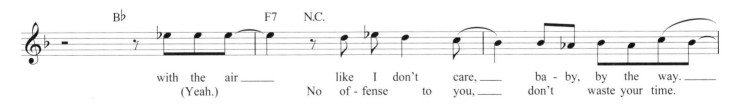

___ you feel like a room with - out a roof. _____ (Be - cause I'm

hap - py.) Clap a - long if _____ you feel ___ like hap - pi - ness is the truth. _

___ (Be - cause I'm hap - py.) Clap a - long _____ if _____ you know what

hap - pi - ness is to you. ___ (Be - cause I'm hap - py.) Clap a - long if ___

___ you feel ___ like that's what you wan - na do. ___

𝄋 Bridge

Bring me down, _____ can't noth - in' bring me down; _

_____ your love is too high. Bring me down, _____ can't noth - in'

44

bring me down. _____ (Let me tell you now.) _ I said... (Be - cause I'm

Chorus

hap - py.) Clap a - long if _____ you feel like a room with - out a roof. _

(Be - cause I'm hap - py.) Clap a - long if _____ you feel ___ like

hap - pi - ness is the truth. ___ (Be - cause I'm hap - py.) Clap a - long _____ if ___

___ you know what hap - pi - ness is to you. ___ (Be - cause I'm

4th time, To Coda

hap - py.) Clap a - long if _____ you feel ___ like that's what you wan - na do. _

D.S. al Coda   **Coda**

___ (Be - cause I'm ___   ___

Hall of Fame

Words and Music by Danny O'Donoghue, Mark Sheehan, James Barry, Andrew Frampton and Will Adams

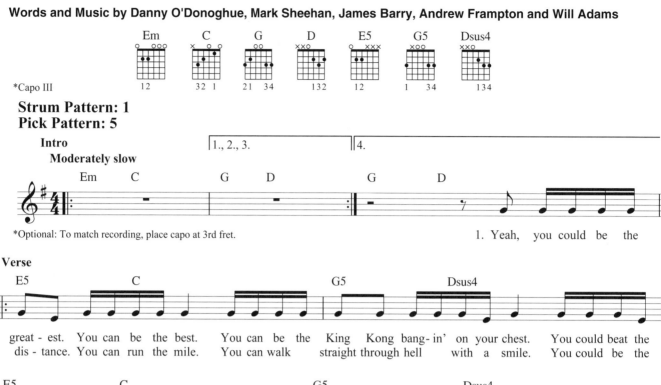

*Capo III

Strum Pattern: 1
Pick Pattern: 5

Intro
Moderately slow

*Optional: To match recording, place capo at 3rd fret.

1. Yeah, you could be the

Verse

great - est. You can be the best. You can be the King Kong bang-in' on your chest. You could beat the
dis - tance. You can run the mile. You can walk straight through hell with a smile. You could be the

world. You could beat the war. You could talk to God, go bang-in' on His door. You can throw your
he - ro. You could get the gold, break-ing all the rec-ords they thought nev - er could be broke. Do it for your

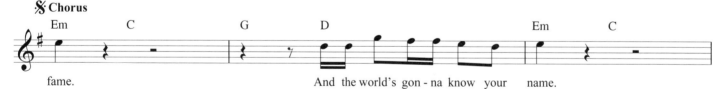

hands up. You can beat the clock. You can move a moun - tain. You can break rocks. You could be a
peo - ple, do it for your pride. Nev - er gon - na know if you nev - er e - ven try. Do it for your

mas - ter, don't wait for luck. Ded - i - cate your - self and you could find your - self stand-in' in the hall of
coun - try, do it for your name. 'Cause there gon - na be a day when you're

§ Chorus

fame. And the world's gon - na know your name.

'Cause you burn with the bright-est flame. And the world's gon - na know your

name. And you'll be on the walls of the hall of fame. 2. You can go the

Ho Hey

Words and Music by Jeremy Fraites and Wesley Schultz

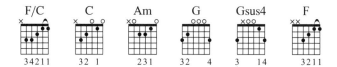

Strum Pattern: 5
Pick Pattern: 1

Intro
Moderately slow, in 2

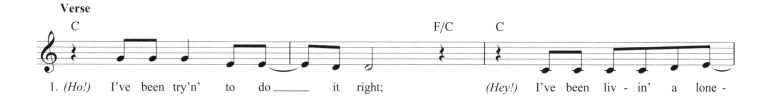

Shouted: (Ho!)   *Hey!)*

*Lyrics in italics are shouted throughout.

Verse

1. *(Ho!)* I've been try'n' to do ____ it right;   *(Hey!)* I've been liv-in' a lone-

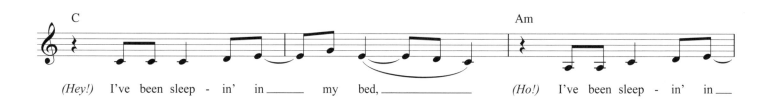

-ly life. _____ *(Ho!)* I've been sleep-in' here ____ in-stead;

(Hey!) I've been sleep-in' in ____ my bed, _____ *(Ho!)* I've been sleep-in' in ____ my bed. _____ *(Hey!*   *Ho!)*

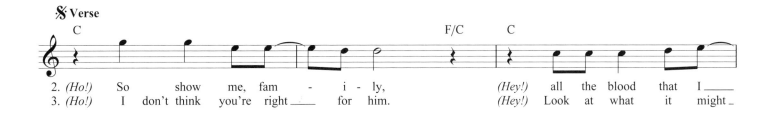

𝄋 Verse

2. (Ho!) So show me, fam - i - ly, (Hey!) all the blood that I _____
3. (Ho!) I don't think you're right _____ for him. (Hey!) Look at what it might _

___ will bleed. (Ho!) I don't know where I _____ be - long,
___ have been _____ if you (Ho!) took a bus to Chi - na town.

(Hey!) I don't know where I _____ went wrong, _____ (Ho!) but I can write _
(Hey!) I'd be stand - in' on _____ Ca - nal _____ (Ho!) and Bow -

To Coda 1 ⊕

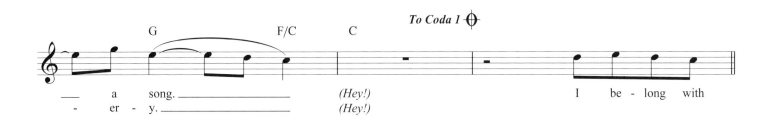

___ a song. _____ (Hey!) I be - long with
- er - y. _____ (Hey!)

𝄋 𝄋 Chorus
Double-time feel

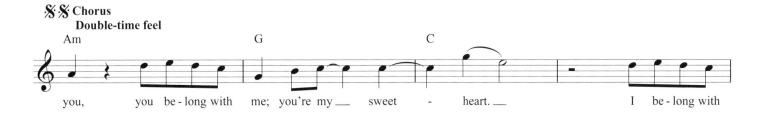

you, you be - long with me; you're my _ sweet - heart. _ I be - long with

End double-time feel

you, you be - long with me; you're my _ sweet... (Ho!

To Coda 2 ⊕   **D.S. al Coda 1**

Hey! Ho! Hey!)

Coda 1

Am   G   F/C

(Ho!) And she'd be stand - in' next _____ to me.

Chorus
Double-time feel

C   Am   G

(Hey!) I be - long with you, you be - long with me; you're my ___ sweet -

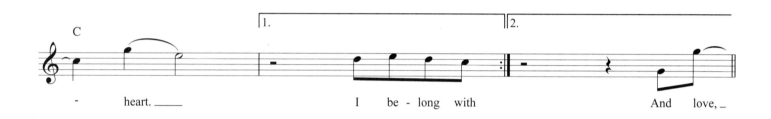

C

1.   2.

- heart. _____ I be - long with   And love, _

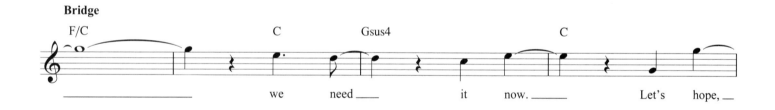

Bridge

F/C   C   Gsus4   C

_____ we need ___ it now. _____ Let's hope, __

F/C   C   Gsus4   F

_____ for some, __   'cause oh, _____

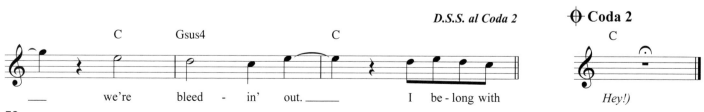

D.S.S. al Coda 2   **Coda 2**

C   Gsus4   C   C

__ we're bleed - in' out. _____ I be - long with   *Hey!)*

How to Save a Life

Words and Music by Joseph King and Isaac Slade

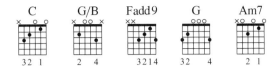

*Tune down 1 step:
(low to high): D-G-C-F-A-D

Strum Pattern: 5
Pick Pattern: 1

Intro
Moderately

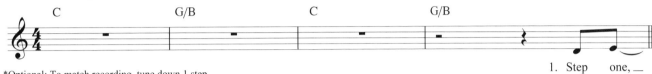

*Optional: To match recording, tune down 1 step.

1. Step one, —

Verse

— you say we need — to talk. He walks, you say, — "Sit

down, it's just — a talk." — He smiles po - lite - ly back at you.

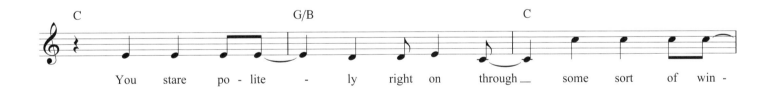

You stare po - lite - ly right on through — some sort of win -

- dow to your right, — as he — goes left and you — stay

right be - tween — the lines — of fear and blame. — You be - gin to won -

Chorus

- der why __ you came. Where / where did I __ go wrong? I lost __ a friend __

__ some - where _ a - long __ in the bit - ter - ness. And I would have __ stayed

up with you __ all night __ had I __ known how to save __ a life. _

Interlude

_

*2nd time, substitute Am7.

Verse

2. Let him know __ that you __ know best __ 'cause
3. As he be - gins __ to raise __ his voice, __ you

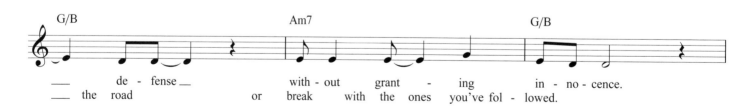

af - ter all __ you do know best. ____ Try to slip past his __
low - er yours _ and grant him one last choice. Drive un - til you lose _

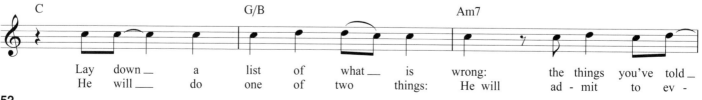

__ de - fense __ with - out grant - ing in - no - cence.
__ the road or break with the ones you've fol - lowed.

Lay down __ a list of what __ is wrong: the things you've told __
He will __ do one of two things: He will ad - mit to ev -

Home

Words and Music by Greg Holden and Drew Pearson

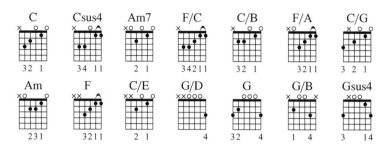

Strum Pattern: 1
Pick Pattern: 5

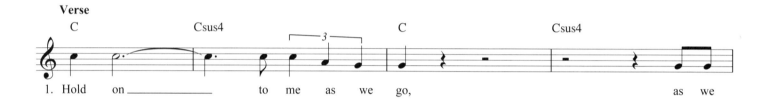

1. Hold on _____ to me as we go,   as we

roll down _____ this un-fa-mil-iar road.   And al-though this

wave _____ is string-ing us a-long,   just

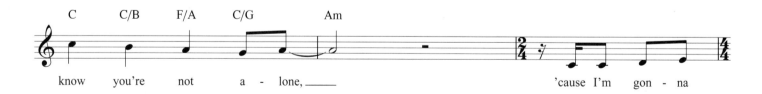

know you're not a-lone, _____   'cause I'm gon-na

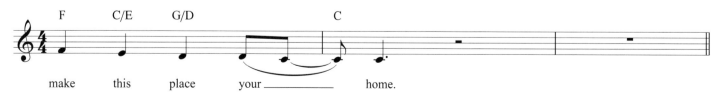

make this place your _____ home.

Verse

2., 3. Set - tle down, _____ it -'ll all be _____ clear.

Don't pay no mind to the de - mons; they fill you with fear.

Trou - ble, it might drag you down. You get lost, you can al - ways be found. Just

know you're not a - lone, _____ 'cause I'm gon - na

make this place your _____ home.

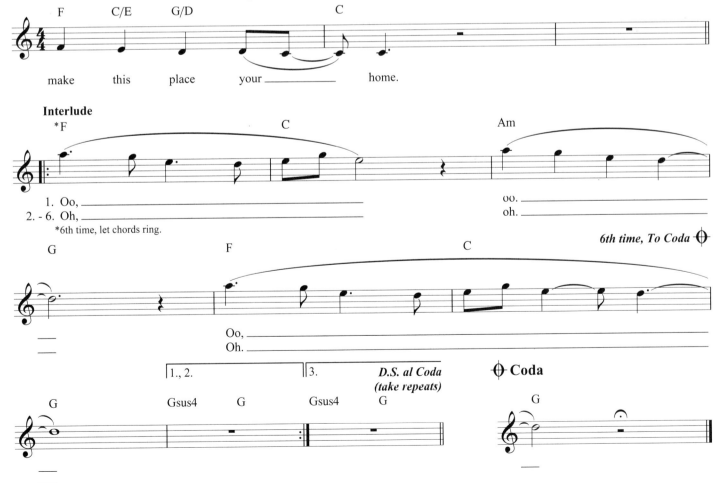

Interlude

1. Oo, _____ oo. _____
2. - 6. Oh, _____ oh. _____

*6th time, let chords ring.

6th time, To Coda

Oo, _____
Oh. _____

1., 2.   3.   *D.S. al Coda (take repeats)*   Coda

Human

Words and Music by Christina Perri and Martin Johnson

I Gotta Feeling

Words and Music by Will Adams, Allan Pineda, Jaime Gomez, Stacy Ferguson, David Guetta and Frederic Riesterer

Strum Pattern: 1
Pick Pattern: 1

good night. A feel - good night. I feel... 1., 5. To-night's the night.

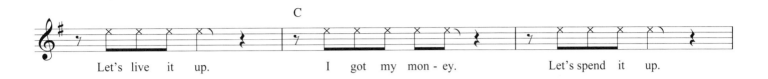

Let's live it up. I got my mon - ey. Let's spend it up.

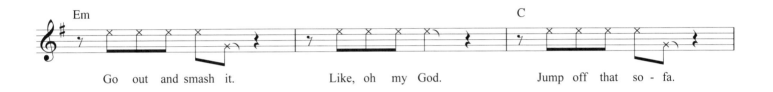

Go out and smash it. Like, oh my God. Jump off that so - fa.

1st time only

Verse

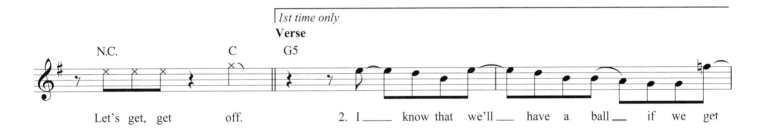

Let's get, get off. 2. I ___ know that we'll ___ have a ball ___ if we get

___ down and go ___ out and just ___ lose it all. ___ I feel stressed ___ out. I wan -

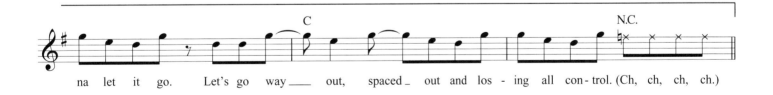

na let it go. Let's go way ___ out, spaced ___ out and los - ing all con - trol. (Ch, ch, ch, ch.)

Verse

3., 6. Fill up my cup. Maz - el tov! Look at her danc - ing;

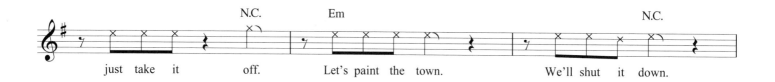

just take it off. Let's paint the town. We'll shut it down.

Let's burn the roof and then we'll do it a - gain. _____ 4., 7. Let's do it, let's

do it, let's do it, let's do it, ___ and do it, and do it, let's live it up and

do it, and do it, and do it, do it, do it. Let's do it. Let's do it. Let's

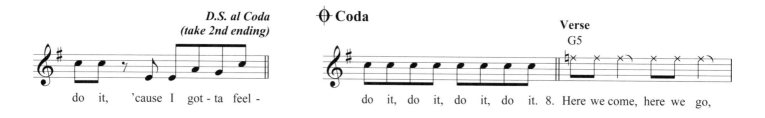

do it, 'cause I got - ta feel -   do it, do it, do it, do it. 8. Here we come, here we go,

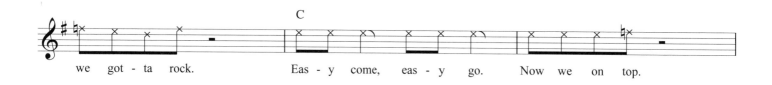

we got - ta rock. Eas - y come, eas - y go. Now we on top.

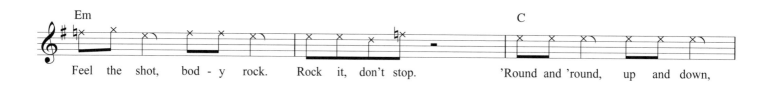

Feel the shot, bod - y rock. Rock it, don't stop. 'Round and 'round, up and down,

a - round the clock. 9. Mon - day, Tues - day, Wednes - day and Thurs - day.

Fri - day, Sat - ur - day, Sat - ur - day to Sun - day. Get, get, get, get, get with us.

You know what we say, say. Par - ty ev - 'ry day. P - p - p - par - ty ev - 'ry day. And I'm feel -

Outro-Chorus

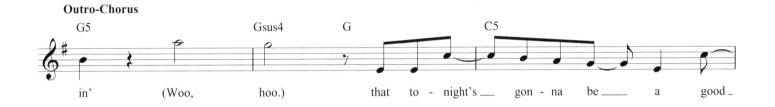

in' (Woo, hoo.) that to - night's __ gon - na be __ a good __

__ night, that to - night's __ gon - na be __ a good __ night, __ that to - night's _

__ gon - na be __ a good, __ good night. __ A feel - in' (Woo,

hoo.) that to - night's __ gon - na be __ a good __ night, that to - night's _

__ gon - na be __ a good __ night, __ that to - night's __ gon - na be __ a good, _

__ good night. __ (Woo, hoo.)

*Let chord ring.

I Will Follow You Into the Dark

Words and Music by Benjamin Gibbard

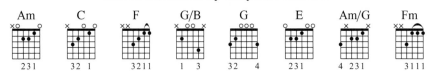

*Capo V

Strum Pattern: 5
Pick Pattern: 1

Intro
Fast

*Optional: To match recording, place capo at 5th fret.

Verse

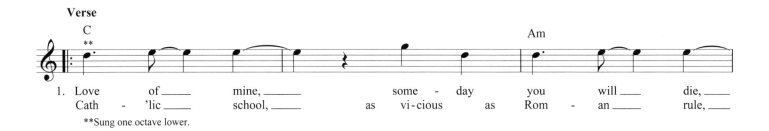

1. Love of ___ mine, ___ some - day you will ___ die, ___
Cath - 'lic ___ school, ___ as vi - cious as Rom - an ___ rule, ___

**Sung one octave lower.

___ but I'll be close be - hind. I'll fol - low you ___
___ I got my knuck - les ___ bruised by a la -

___ in - to the dark. ___ No blind - ing ___ light ___
- dy in black. ___ And I held my ___ tongue ___

Verse

3. You and ___ me, ___ have seen ev - 'ry - thing to ___ see ___

from Bang - kok to Cal - ga - ry, ___ and the soles ___

of your shoes ___ are all worn ___ down. ___

The time ___ for sleep is ___ now, ___ but it's noth - ing to

cry a - bout ___ 'cause we'll hold ___ each - oth - er soon ___

in the black - est ___ of rooms. _____

D.S. al Coda 2

If

⊕ Coda

And I'll fol - low you in - to the dark.

*Let chords ring.

The Lazy Song

Words and Music by Bruno Mars, Ari Levine, Philip Lawrence and Keinan Warsame

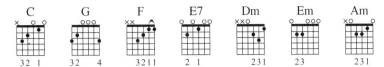

*Tune down 1/2 step
(low to high) E♭-A♭-D♭-G♭-B♭-E♭

Strum Pattern: 1
Pick Pattern: 5

Chorus
Moderately slow, in 2

To - day I don't feel like do - in' an - y - thing.

*Optional: To match recording, tune down 1/2 step.

I just wan - na lay in my bed. _____ Don't

feel like pick - in' up _____ my phone, so leave a mes - sage at the tone 'cause to -

day I swear I'm not do - in' an - y - thing. 1. I'm gon - na

Verse

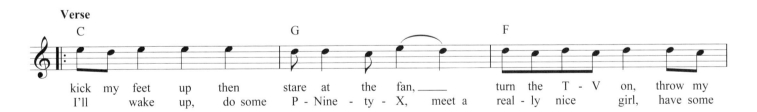

kick my feet up then stare at the fan, _____ turn the T - V on, throw my
I'll wake up, do some P - Nine - ty - X, meet a real - ly nice girl, have some

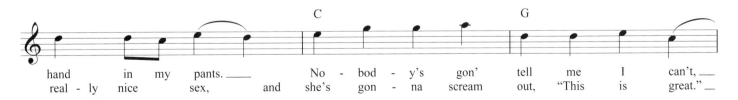

hand in my pants. _____ No - bod - y's gon' tell me I can't, _____
real - ly nice sex, and she's gon - na scream out, "This is great." _____

no.   I'll be loung - in' on the couch,   just
Yeah,   I might mess a - round and get my

chill - in' in my Snug - gie,   click to M - T - V so they can teach me how to doug - ie, 'cause
col - lege de - gree.   I bet my old man will be so proud of me.   Well,

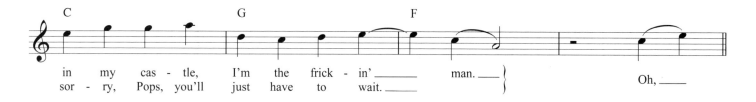

in my cas - tle,   I'm the frick - in' _____ man. ___
sor - ry, Pops, you'll just have to wait. _____   Oh, ___

Pre-Chorus

yes, I said it,   I said it, I said it 'cause __ I

𝄋 **Chorus**

can. __   To - day I don't feel like do - in' an - y - thing.

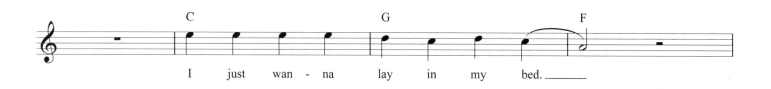

I just wan - na lay in my bed. _____

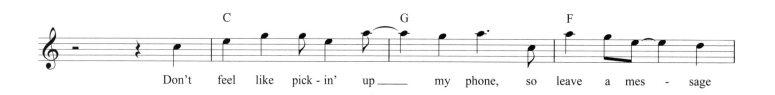

Don't feel like pick - in' up _____ my phone, so leave a mes - sage

at the tone 'cause to - day I swear I'm not do - in' an -

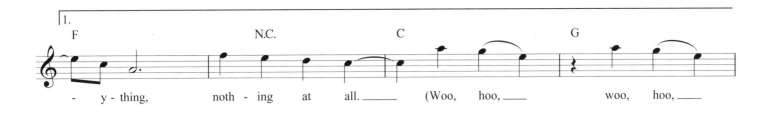

- y - thing, noth - ing at all. _____ (Woo, hoo, _____ woo, hoo, _____

To Coda ⊕

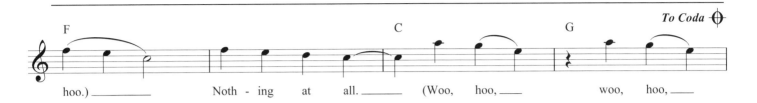

hoo.) _____ Noth - ing at all. _____ (Woo, hoo, _____ woo, hoo, _____

hoo.) _____ 2. To - mor - row - y - thing, No, I

Bridge

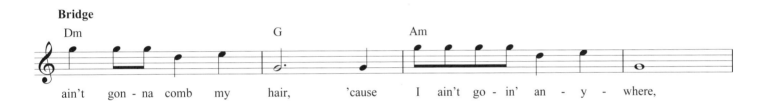

ain't gon - na comb my hair, 'cause I ain't go - in' an - y - where,

no, no, no, no, no, no, no, _____ no, no, oh. I'll just

strut in my birth - day suit and let ev - 'ry - thing_ hang loose. _____

D.S. al Coda
(take 1st ending)

Yeah, yeah, yeah, yeah, yeah, yeah, yeah,_ yeah, yeah, yeah. Oh, _____ to -

⊕ **Coda**

hoo.) _____ Noth - ing at all. _____

Jar of Hearts

Words and Music by Barrett Yeretsian, Christina Perri and Drew Lawrence

are?   are?   **Bridge** And it took so long just to

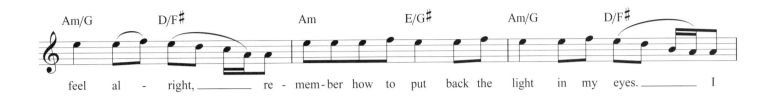

feel al - right, _____ re - mem-ber how to put back the light in my eyes. _____ I

wish I had missed the first time that we kissed _____ 'cause you broke all ____ your

prom - is - es. ____ And now your back, _ you don't get to get me back. _____

Chorus

all. ____ } And who do you think you are, run-ning 'round leav - ing scars, ___ col - lect-ing your jar of

hearts and tear-ing love a - part? ____ You're gon - na catch a cold ____ from the ice in - side your

Outro

soul. _____ So don't come back _ for me, don't come back _ at all.

Who do you think you _____ are? Who do you think you are?

Jealousy

Words and Music by Natalie Merchant

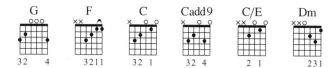

Strum Pattern: 5
Pick Pattern: 1

Chorus
Moderately

Oo, _____ jeal-ous-y.

Oo, _____ jeal-ous-

y.
1. Is she ___ fine, so well-bred, the per-fect
2. Is she ___ bright, so well-read, are there

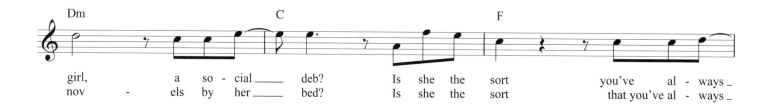

girl, a so-cial ___ deb? Is she the sort you've al-ways ___
nov-els by her ___ bed? Is she the sort that you've al-ways ___

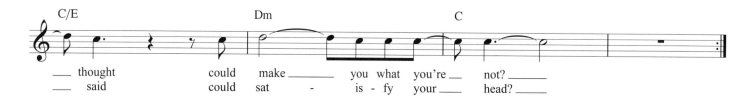

___ thought could make ___ you what you're ___ not? ___
___ said could sat-is-fy your ___ head? ___

Chorus

Oo, _____ jeal-ous-y.

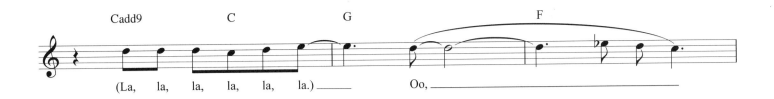

Cadd9   C   G   F

(La, la, la, la, la, la.) _____ Oo, _____

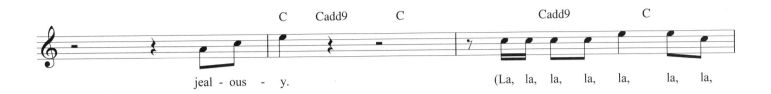

C Cadd9   C   Cadd9   C

jeal - ous - y.   (La, la, la, la, la, la, la,

G   F   C Cadd9   C

la.) Oo, _____   my jeal - ous - y.

Outro-Verse

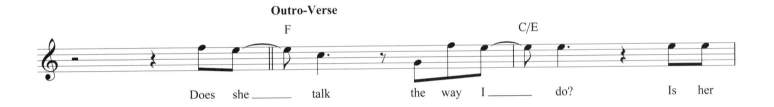

F   C/E

Does she _____ talk the way I _____ do?   Is her

Dm   C   F

voice _____ re - mind - ing _____ you   'bout the prom - is - es,   the lit - tle white lies _

C/E   Dm   C   F

_ too? Some - times,   tell me, while she's touch - ing you,   just by mis -

C/E   Dm   C
           rit.

take,   ac - ci - dent - ly do you say my _____ name?

Lego House

Words and Music by Ed Sheeran, Chris Leonard and Jake Gosling

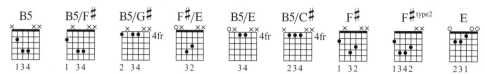

Strum Pattern: 3
Pick Pattern: 1

Intro
Moderately slow, in 2

Verse

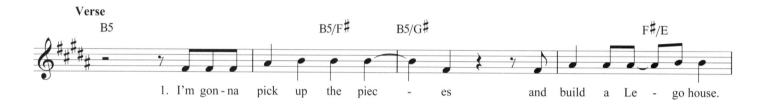

1. I'm gon-na pick up the piec - es and build a Le - go house.

If things go wrong, we can knock it down.

My three words have two mean - ings, but there's one thing on ___ my mind.

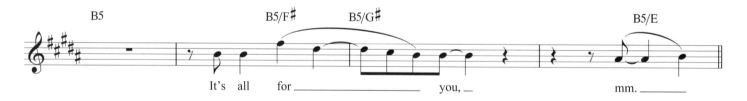

It's all for ___ you, ___ mm. ___

Pre-Chorus

And it's dark in a cold De - cem - ber, but I've got you to keep me warm. ___

If you're bro - ken, I will mend ya,

*2nd time, substitute B5/E.

and I'll keep you shel-tered from the storm that's _ rag - ing on, _____ now.

*2nd time, substitute F#/E.

𝄋 Chorus

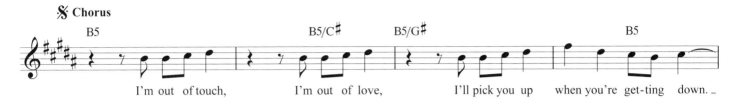

I'm out of touch, I'm out of love, I'll pick you up when you're get-ting down. _

___ And out of all these things I've done, I think I love you bet-ter now.

I'm out of sight, I'm out of mind. I'll do it all for you in time. __

2nd time, To Coda 1 𝄌

3rd time, To Coda 2 𝄌

___ And out of all these things I've done, I think I love you bet-ter now.

Now. _____

Verse

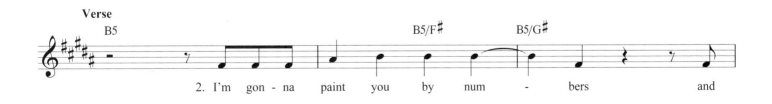

2. I'm gon - na paint you by num - bers and

col - our you ___ in. If things go right, we can

frame it and put you on a wall. _____ And it's

so hard to say _____ it, but I've been here be - fore. _____

D.S. al Coda 1

_____ Now I'll sur - ren - der up _____ my heart and swap it for yours. _____

Coda 1

Bridge

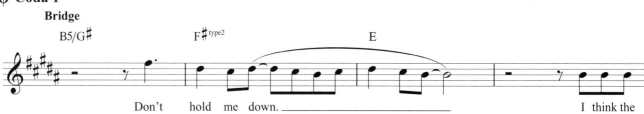

Don't hold me down. _____ I think the

brac - es are break - ing and it's more than I _____ can take. _____

D.S.S. al Coda 2 ## Coda 2

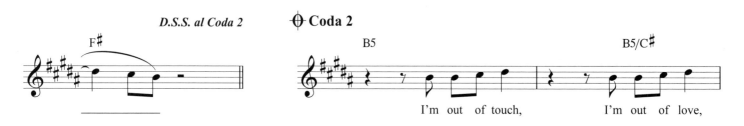

I'm out of touch, I'm out of love,

I'll pick you up when you're get - ting down. And out of

all these things I've done, I will love you bet - ter now.

Let Her Go

Words and Music by Michael David Rosenberg

*Capo VII

Strum Pattern: 1
Pick Pattern: 5

Intro
Slow

*Optional: To match recording, place capo at 7th fret.

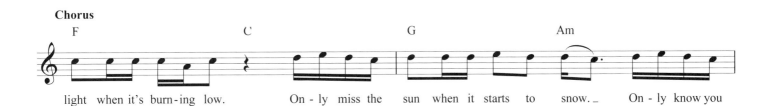

Well, you on - ly need the
**Sung one octave lower throughout.

Chorus

light when it's burn-ing low. On - ly miss the sun when it starts to snow._ On - ly know you

love her when you let her go. On - ly know you've been

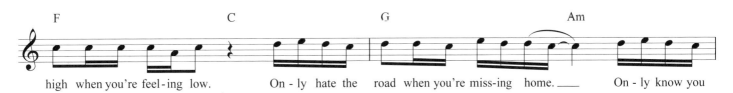

high when you're feel-ing low. On - ly hate the road when you're miss-ing home. ____ On - ly know you

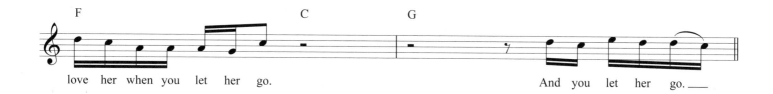

love her when you let her go. And you let her go. ___

Interlude

Verse

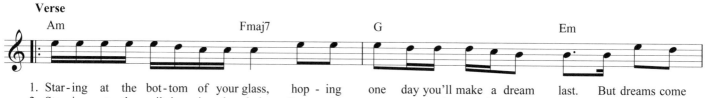

1. Star-ing at the bot-tom of your glass, hop-ing one day you'll make a dream last. But dreams come
2. Star-ing at the ceil-ing in the dark. Same old emp-ty feel - ing in your heart, 'cause love comes

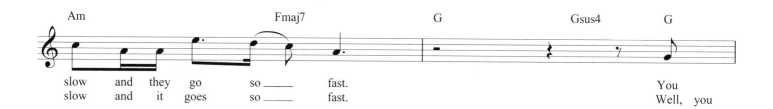

slow and they go so ___ fast. You
slow and it goes so ___ fast. Well, you

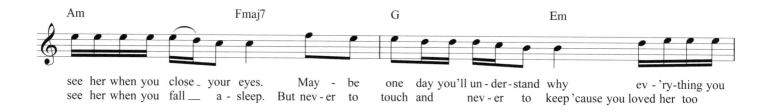

see her when you close ___ your eyes. May - be one day you'll un-der-stand why ev-'ry-thing you
see her when you fall ___ a - sleep. But nev - er to touch and nev - er to keep 'cause you loved her too

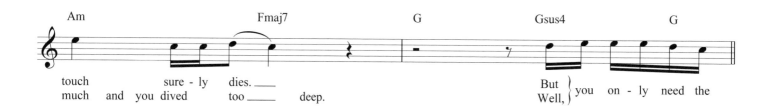

touch sure - ly dies. ___ But you on - ly need the
much and you dived too ___ deep. Well, you on - ly need the

𝄉 Chorus

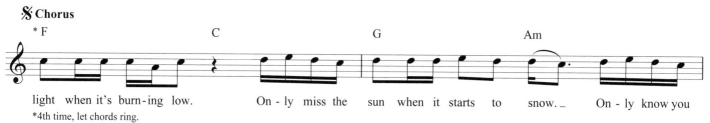

light when it's burn-ing low. On - ly miss the sun when it starts to snow. ___ On - ly know you
*4th time, let chords ring.

76

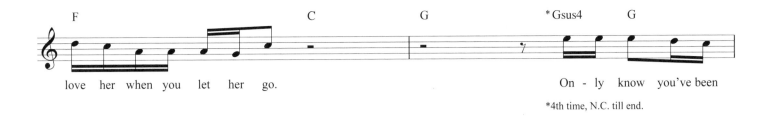

love her when you let her go.

On - ly know you've been

*4th time, N.C. till end.

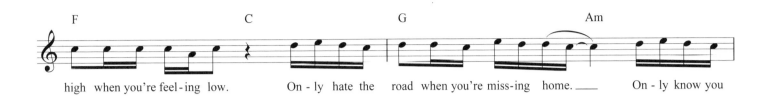

high when you're feel - ing low.
On - ly hate the road when you're miss - ing home. ____
On - ly know you

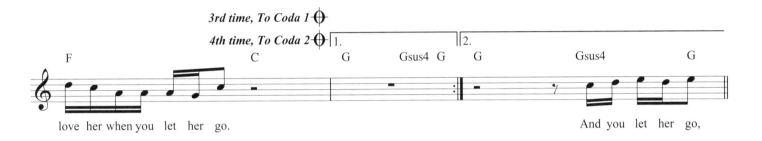

3rd time, To Coda 1
4th time, To Coda 2

love her when you let her go.

And you let her go,

Bridge

oh, oh, ____ oh, no.
And you let her go, oh, oh, ____ oh,

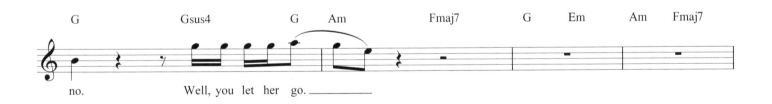

no. Well, you let her go. _____

D.S. al Coda 1 **Coda 1** **D.S. al Coda 2**

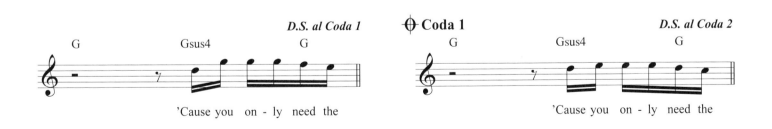

'Cause you on - ly need the
'Cause you on - ly need the

Coda 2

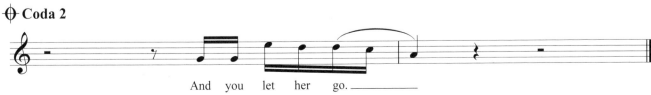

And you let her go. _____

Let It Go

from Disney's Animated Feature FROZEN

Music and Lyrics by Kristen Anderson-Lopez and Robert Lopez

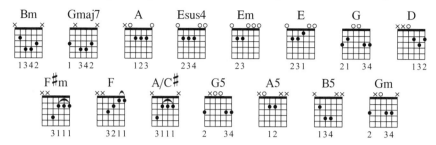

*Capo VI

Strum Pattern: 3
Pick Pattern: 5

Intro
Moderately slow, in 2

*Optional: To match recording, place capo at 6th fret.

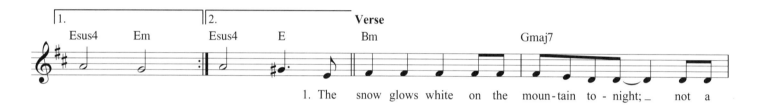

1. The snow glows white on the moun-tain to - night; _ not a

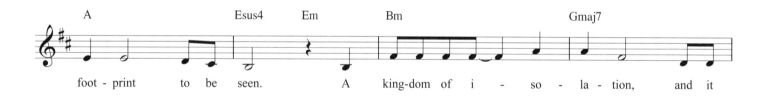

foot - print to be seen. A king-dom of i - so - la - tion, and it

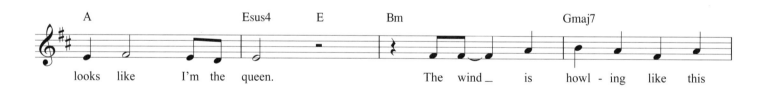

looks like I'm the queen. The wind _ is howl - ing like this

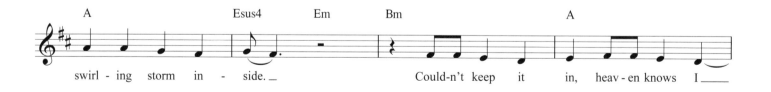

swirl - ing storm in - side. _ Could-n't keep it in, heav - en knows I _

Pre-Chorus

_ tried. Don't let _ them in, don't let them

see; be the good girl you al-ways have _ to be. Con - ceal, _ don't feel, don't let _ them

know... _____ Well, now _____ they know. _____ Let it

𝄋 Chorus

go, let it go; can't hold it back an - y - more. Let it
go, let it go; I am one with the wind and sky. Let it

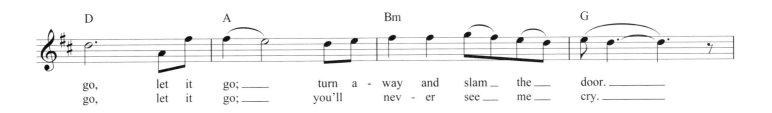

go, let it go; _____ turn a - way and slam _ the _ door.
go, let it go; _____ you'll nev - er see _ me _ cry. _____

I don't _ care _____ what they're go - ing to _____ say; _____ let the
Here I _____ stand, _____ and here I'll _ stay; _____ let the

To Coda ⊕

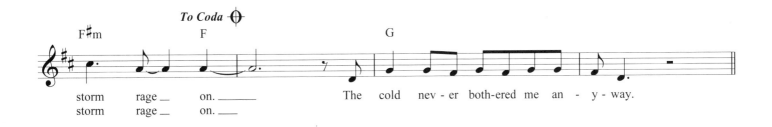

storm rage _ on. _____ The cold nev - er both-ered me an - y - way.
storm rage _ on. _____

Verse

2. It's fun - ny how some dis - tance makes

ev - 'ry - thing __ seem small; and the fears that once __ con - trolled me can't

Pre-Chorus

get to me __ at all. It's time __ to see what I can

do, to test __ the lim - its and break through. No right, __ no wrong, no rules for

D.S. al Coda **Coda**

me, I'm free! _____ Let it __

Bridge

My pow - er

flur - ries through the air in - to the ground. My soul __ is

spi - ral - ing in fro - zen frac - tals all a - round. __ And one __ thought

cry - stal - li - zes like an i - cy blast: I'm nev - er

go - ing back; the past is in the past! Let it

Outro-Chorus

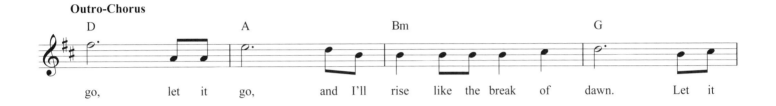

go, let it go, and I'll rise like the break of dawn. Let it

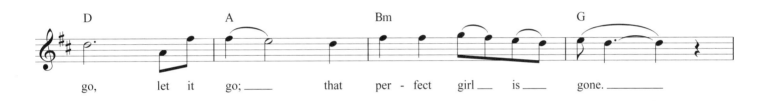

go, let it go; that per - fect girl is gone.

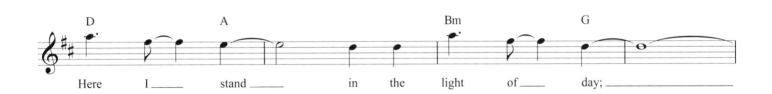

Here I stand in the light of day;

let the storm rage on. The

cold nev - er both - ered me an - y - way.

81

Little Talks

Words and Music by Of Monsters And Men

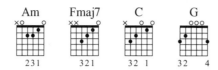

*Capo I

Strum Pattern: 5
Pick Pattern: 1

Intro
Very fast

*Optional: To match recording, place capo at 1st fret.

**Shouted: (Hey!)

**Lyrics in italics are shouted throughout.

Hey!

Hey!)

Verse

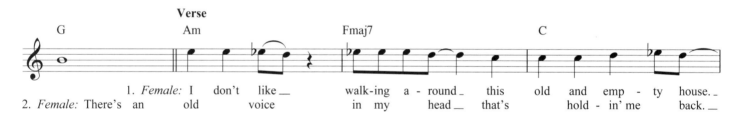

1. *Female:* I don't like ___ walk-ing a - round ___ this old and emp - ty house. ___
2. *Female:* There's an old voice in my head ___ that's hold - in' me back. ___

___ *Male:* So hold my hand, I'll walk with you, ___ my dear.
___ *Male:* Well, tell her that I miss our lit - tle talks.

Female: The stairs creek as you sleep, ___ it's keep - ing me a - wake. ___
Female: Soon it will be o - ver ___ and bur - ied with our ___

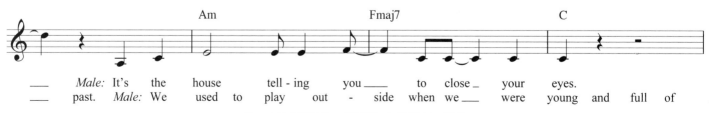

___ *Male:* It's the house tell - ing you ___ to close ___ your eyes.
___ past. *Male:* We used to play out - side when we ___ were young and full of

Verse

gone, gone, gone a - way. ___ I watched you dis - ap - pear. ___ All that's left

*Let chord ring.

is a ghost ___ of you. Now we're torn, torn, torn a - part. ___ There's

**Strum chord and let ring.

noth - ing we can do. ___ Just let me go. We'll meet a - gain ___ soon.

***Strum chord and let ring.

Now, wait, wait, wait for ___ me. Please hang a - round. ___

†Strum half notes.

D.S. al Coda 1

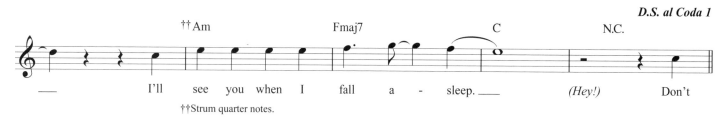

___ I'll see you when I fall a - sleep. ___ *(Hey!)* Don't

††Strum quarter notes.

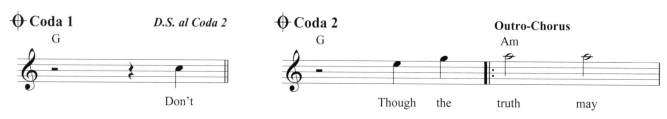

$\oplus$ **Coda 1**   *D.S. al Coda 2* $\oplus$ **Coda 2**   **Outro-Chorus**

Don't   Though the truth may

var - y, this ___ ship ___ will car - ry our ___ bod - ies

safe to ___ shore. Though the

84

Lucky

Words and Music by Jason Mraz, Colbie Caillat and Timothy Fagan

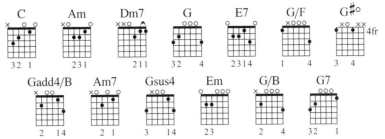

Strum Pattern: 3
Pick Pattern: 3

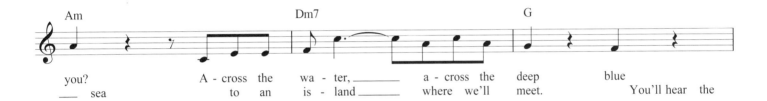

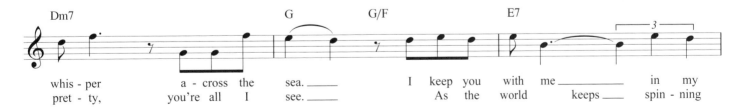

Chorus

Both: Luck - y I'm in ___ love with my best friend, luck - y to have ___

___ been where I have been. Luck - y to be com - ing home a -

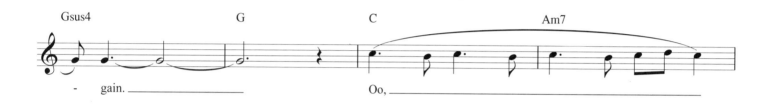

- gain. ___ Oo, ___

Bridge

oo. ___

*{ Female: They don't know how long it takes,

Male: They don't know how long it

*Sung at once.

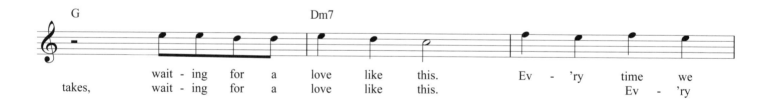

takes, wait - ing for a love like this. Ev - 'ry time we

wait - ing for a love like this. Ev - 'ry

say good - bye, *Both:* I wish we had one more kiss. I'll

time we say good - bye, }

wait for you, I prom - ise you I will. ___ I'm ___

𝄋 𝄋 Chorus

Both: { luck - y / Luck - y } I'm in ___ love with my best friend, luck - y to have ___ been where I have

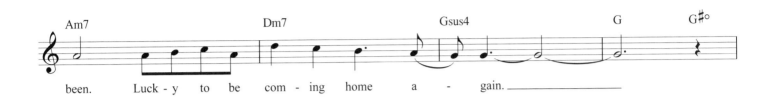

been. Luck - y to be com - ing home a - gain. ___

Luck - y we're in ___ love in ev - 'ry way, luck - y to have ___ stayed where we have

To Coda 2 ⊕

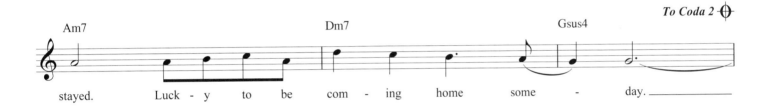

stayed. Luck - y to be com - ing home some - day. ___

D.S. al Coda 1 ⊕ **Coda 1** ***D.S.S. al Coda 2*** ⊕ **Coda 2**

___ 2. *Male:* And so I'm here, right now. ___

Outro

Oo, ___ oo. ___

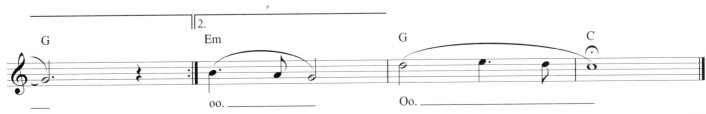

___ oo. ___ Oo. ___

87

Makes Me Wonder

Words by Adam Levine
Music by Adam Levine, Jesse Carmichael and Mickey Madden

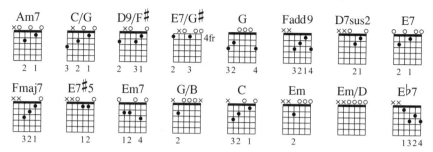

*Capo II

Strum Pattern: 3
Pick Pattern: 3

Intro
Moderately

*Optional: To match recording, place capo at 2nd fret.
**Chord symbols reflect implied harmony.

Verse

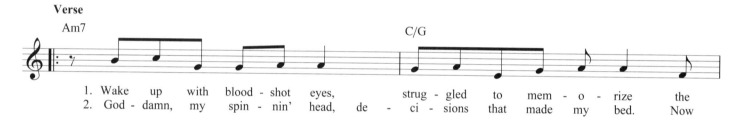

1. Wake up with blood-shot eyes, strug-gled to mem-o-rize the
2. God-damn, my spin-nin' head, de-ci-sions that made my bed. Now

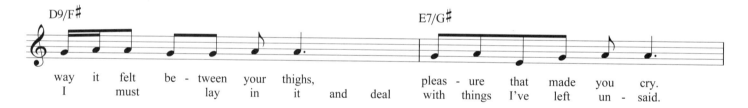

way it felt be-tween your thighs, pleas-ure that made you cry.
I must lay in it and deal with things I've left un-said.

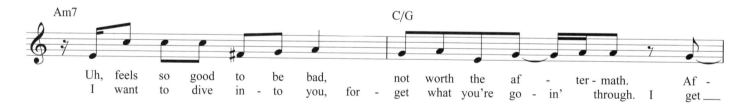

Uh, feels so good to be bad, not worth the af-ter-math. Af-
I want to dive in-to you, for-get what you're go-in' through. I get ___

-ter that, af-ter that, try ___ to get you back.
__ be-hind; make ___ your move. For-get ___ a-bout the truth. I

Pre-Chorus

still don't have a rea-son, and you don't have the time. _

G   Am7   G   Fadd9   G   E7/G#

And it real-ly makes me won-der if I ev-er gave a fuck a-bout

𝄋 **Chorus**

Am7   C/G   D7sus2

you. Give me some-thin' to be-lieve in 'cause I don't be-lieve in you an-y-

E7   E7/G#   Am7   1.   C/G

more, an-y-more._____ I won-der if it e-ven makes a dif-f'rence to try.__

Fmaj7   E7#5   2.   C/G

__ Yeah, so this is good-bye.   e-ven makes a dif-f'rence, it

Fmaj7   E7   E7/G#   Am7

e-ven makes a dif-f'rence to try,____ yeah.__   And you told me how you're

C/G   D7sus2   E7   E7/G#

feel-in', but I don't be-lieve it's true an-y-more, an-y-more._____

To Coda ⊕

Am7   C/G   Fmaj7

I won-der if it e-ven makes a dif-f'rence to cry,_____ oh no,

89

Bridge

so this is good-bye. I've been here be-fore. One day I'll wake up and it

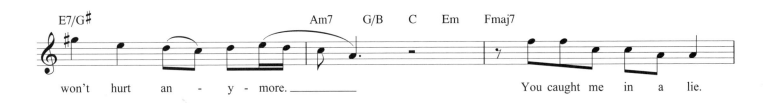

won't hurt an - y - more. ___ You caught me in a lie.

I have no al - i - bi. The words you say don't have a mean - ing 'cause ___ I

Pre-Chorus

still don't have a rea - son, and you don't have the time. ___ And it

real - ly makes me won - der if I ev - er gave a fuck a - bout you and I, and

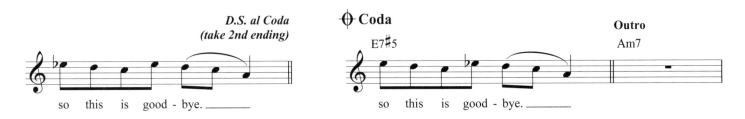

so this is good - bye. ___ so this is good - bye. ___

So this is good - bye. ___ Yeah, so this is good - bye. ___

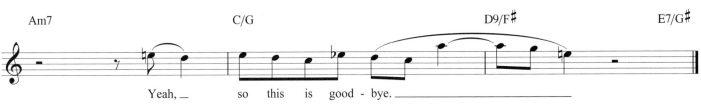

Yeah, ___ so this is good - bye. ___

Man on Fire

Words and Music by Alexander Ebert

*Capo IV

Strum Pattern: 1
Pick Pattern: 5

Intro
Moderately slow, in 2

*Optional: To match recording, place capo at 4th fret

(Mm.)

Chorus

___ I'm a man on fire walk-in' through your street with one gui-

tar and two danc-in' feet. On-ly one de-sire

that's left in me: I want the whole damn world to come dance with

Verse

me. 1. Oh, _____ mm, _____ come dance with

me o-ver mur-der ___ and pain.
me o-ver heart-ache ___ and rage.

Come set you free o-ver heart-ache ___ and shame.
Come set us free o-ver pan-ic ___ and strange.

I wan-na see your bod - ies burn - in' ___ like old, big sun.

I wan-na know what we've been learn - in' ___ and learn - in'

Pre-Chorus

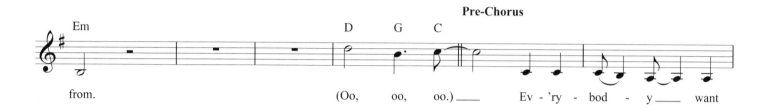

from. (Oo, oo, oo.) ___ Ev - 'ry - bod - y ___ want

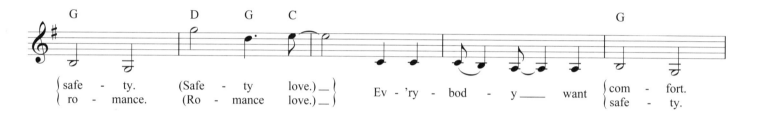

{ safe - ty. (Safe - ty love.) __ }
{ ro - mance. (Ro - mance love.) __ } Ev - 'ry - bod - y ___ want { com - fort.
{ safe - ty.

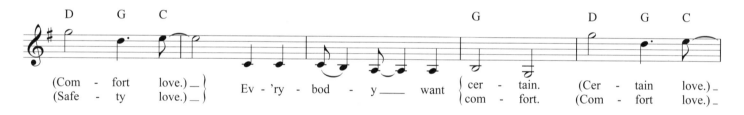

(Com - fort love.) __ }
(Safe - ty love.) __ } Ev - 'ry - bod - y ___ want { cer - tain. (Cer - tain love.) _
{ com - fort. (Com - fort love.) _

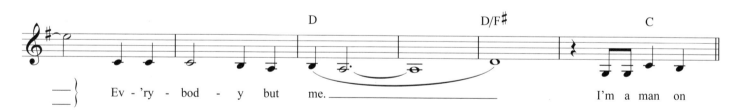

__ }
__ } Ev - 'ry - bod - y but me. ___ I'm a man on

Chorus

fire walk-in' down your street with one gui - tar and two danc - in'

To Coda ⊕

feet. On - ly one de - sire that's { left } in me:
{ still }

92

I want the whole damn world to come dance with me.

Bridge

Ba, da, ba, ba, da, ba, ba, da, ba, ba, da, _____

ba, da, ba, ba, da, ba, ba, da, ba, ba, da, da, da, da.

Ba, da, ba, ba, da, ba, ba, da, ba, ba, da, _____

da, da, da.

Verse

2. Hey, yeah, _ come dance with

D.S. al Coda

Coda

I want the whole damn world to come dance with me.

Outro

The Man Who Can't Be Moved

Words and Music by Stephen Kipner, Andrew Frampton, Mark Sheenan and Danny O'Donaghue

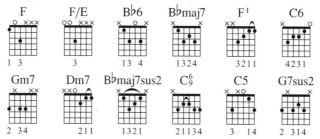

*Capo V

Strum Pattern: 5
Pick Pattern: 5

Intro
Moderately

*Optional: To match recording, place capo at 5th fret.

Verse

1. Go - ing back to the cor - ner where I first saw you, gon -

na camp in my sleep - ing bag, I'm not gon - na move. Got some words on card - board, got

your pic - ture in my hand, say - ing, "If you see this girl, can you tell her where I am?" 2. Some try

Verse

to hand me mon - ey, they don't un - der - stand, I'm not
3. Po - lice - man says, "Son, you can't stay here." I say,

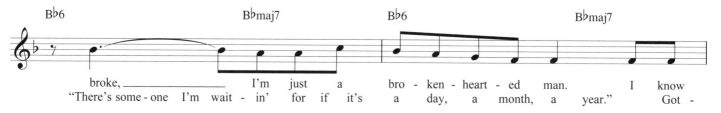

broke, _____ I'm just a bro - ken - heart - ed man. I know
"There's some - one I'm wait - in' for if it's a day, a month, a year." Got -

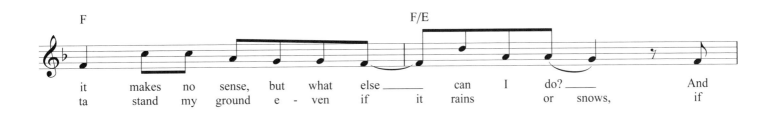

F   F/E

it   makes   no   sense,   but   what   else _____ can   I   do? _____   And
ta   stand   my   ground   e - ven   if   it   rains   or   snows,   if

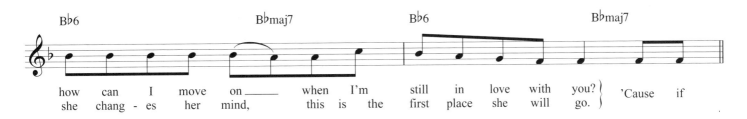

Bb6   Bbmaj7   Bb6   Bbmaj7

how   can   I   move   on _____ when   I'm   still   in   love   with   you? }   'Cause   if
she   chang - es   her   mind,   this   is   the   first   place   she   will   go.

𝄉 Chorus

F¹   C6   Gm7

one   day   you   wake   up   and   find   that   you're   mis - sing   me __   and   you   heart   starts   to   won - der   where   on   this

Bbmaj7   F¹   C6

earth   I   could   be, ___   think - ing   may - be   you'll   come   back   here   to   the   place   that   we'd   meet, _   and   you'll

Gm7   Bbmaj7   F¹

see   me   wait - ing   for   you   on   the   cor - ner   of   the   street.   So   I'm   not _____ mov - in', _____

1.   **Interlude**

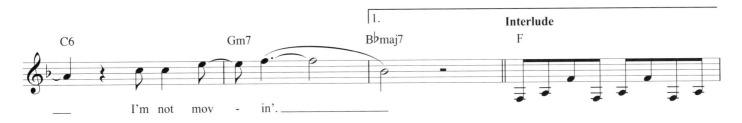

C6   Gm7   Bbmaj7   F

__   I'm   not   mov - in'. _____

F/E   Bb6   Bbmaj7   Bb6   Bbmaj7   N.C.

2.   ***To Coda*** ⊕

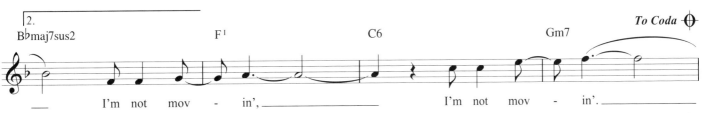

Bbmaj7sus2   F¹   C6   Gm7

__   I'm   not   mov - in', _____   I'm   not   mov - in'. _____

Bridge

People talk a - bout the guy who's wait - ing on a

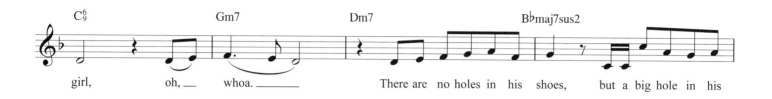

girl, oh, ___ whoa. ___ There are no holes in his shoes, but a big hole in his

world, mm. ___ Well, may - be I'll get fa - mous as the

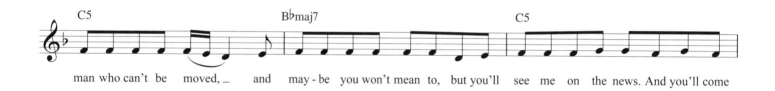

man who can't be moved, _ and may - be you won't mean to, but you'll see me on the news. And you'll come

run - ning to the cor - ner, 'cause you know it's just for ___ you. ___ I'm the man _

D.S. al Coda
(take 2nd ending)

___ who can't be moved. I'm the man ___ who can't be moved. 'Cause if

Coda

Outro-Verse

___ Go - ing back to the cor - ner where

I first saw you, gon - na camp in my sleep - ing bag, I'm not gon - na move. ___

No One

Words and Music by Alicia Keys, Kerry Brothers, Jr. and George Harry

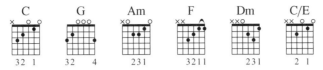

C   G   Am   F   Dm   C/E

*Capo IV

Strum Pattern: 2
Pick Pattern: 2

Intro
Moderately slow

C   G   Am

*Optional: To match recording, place capo at 4th fret.

Verse

F   C   G   Am

1. I just want you close where you can

F   C   G   Am

stay for-ev-er. You can be sure that it will

Pre-Chorus

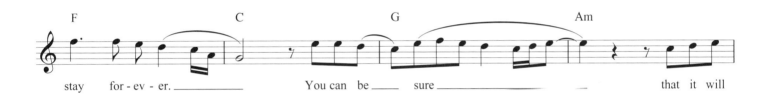

F   C   G

on-ly get bet-ter. You and me to-geth-er through the days and nights.

Am   F   C

I don't wor-ry 'cause ev-'ry-thing's gon-na be al - right. Peo-ple keep talk-in',

G   Am   F

they can say what they like. But all I know is ev-'ry-thing's gon-na be al - right.

Chorus

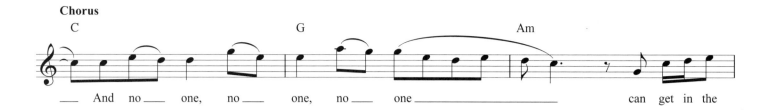

And no — one, no — one, no — one — can get in the

way of what I'm feel - in'. _____ No — one, no — one, no — one _____

_____ can get in the way of what I feel — for you, _____ you, ____

To Coda

— you, _____ can get in the way — of what I feel — for you. —

Verse

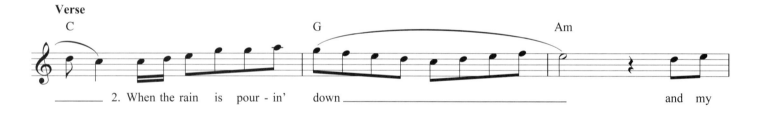

_____ 2. When the rain is pour - in' down _____ and my

heart is hurt - in', — you will al - ways be a - round. _____

D.S. al Coda   **Coda**

_____ This I know for cer - tain. —   __ of what I feel. —   I

Bridge

know ____ some peo - ple search the world to find _____ some - thin' like

what we have. ____ I know ____ peo-ple will try, try to di-vide some-thin' so

Chorus

real. ____ So, 'til the end of time, I'm tell-ing you there ain't no one, ____ no ____

one, no ____ one ____ can get in the way of what I'm feel - in'. ____

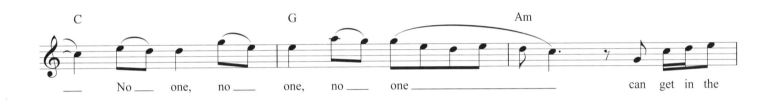

____ No ____ one, no ____ one, no ____ one ____ can get in the

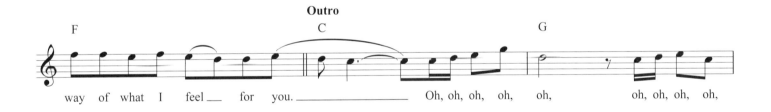

Outro

way of what I feel ____ for you. ____ Oh, oh, oh, oh, oh, oh, oh, oh, oh,

oh, oh, oh, oh, oh, oh, oh, oh, oh, oh. ____ Oh, oh, oh, oh,

oh, oh, oh, oh, oh, oh, oh, oh, oh, oh, oh, oh,

oh. ____

Mirrors

Words and Music by Justin Timberlake, James Fauntleroy,
Jerome Harmon, Tim Mosley, Chris Godbey and Garland Mosley

*Capo I

Strum Pattern: 3
Pick Pattern: 3

*Optional: To match recording, place capo at 1st fret.

Pre-Chorus

'Cause with your hand in my hand _____ and a pock-et full of soul, I can tell you there's no _____

_____ place we could-n't go. Just put your hand on the past, _____ I'll be try'n' to pull you

through. You just got-ta be strong. _____ 'Cause I don't wan-na lose _____ you now. _____

Chorus

_____ I'm look-ing right at the oth-er half of me. The

va-can-cy that sat in my heart _____ is a space _____ that now you hold. _____

_____ Show me how to fight for now. _____ And I'll

tell you, ba-by, it was eas-y com-ing back here to you once I fig-ured it out. _____

You were right ___ here all a - long. ___

It's like you're my mir - ror, (Oh.) ___ my mir - ror star - ing back

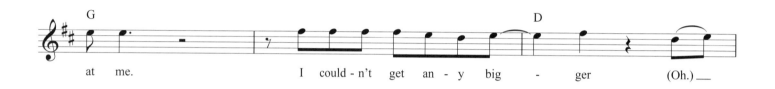

at me. I could - n't get an - y big - ger (Oh.) ___

with an - y - one else be - side of me. And now, it's clear as this prom -

- ise that we're mak - ing, two re - flec - tions in - to one. __

___ 'Cause it's like you're my mir - ror, (Oh.) ___ my mir - ror star - ing back

3rd time, To Coda ⊕

at me, star - ing back at me. 2. Aren't you some - at me.

Bridge

Yes - ter - day is his - to - ry, _____ oh;

to - mor - row's a mys - ter - y, oh. _____

_____ I can see you look - ing back

at me. Keep your eyes on me, ba - by, keep your eyes

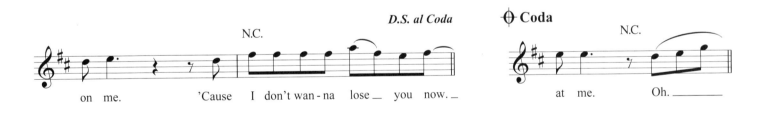

D.S. al Coda   Coda

on me. 'Cause I don't wan - na lose _ you now. _   at me. Oh. _____

Outro

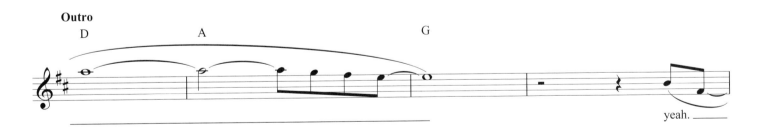

_____   yeah. _____

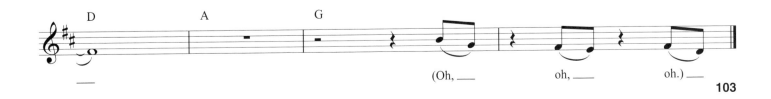

(Oh, _____ oh, _____ oh.) _____

103

Neon Lights

Words and Music by Demi Lovato, Ryan Tedder, Noel Zancanella, Mario Marchetti and Tiffany Vartanyan

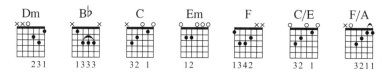

*Capo IV

Strum Pattern: 3
Pick Pattern: 3

Chorus
Moderately

Ba - by, when they look up at ____ the sky, ____ we'll be shoot - ing

*Optional: To match recording, place capo at 4th fret.

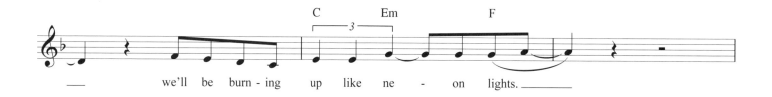

stars just pass - ing by. ____ You'll be com - ing home with me ____ to - night, ____

____ we'll be burn - ing up like ne - on lights. ____

Verse

1., 2. Be still, my heart, 'cause it's freak - ing out, ____

it's freak - ing out, ____ right ____ now. ____ Shin - ing like

stars 'cause we're beau - ti - ful, _____ we're beau - ti - ful, _____ right ___ now. __

Pre-Chorus

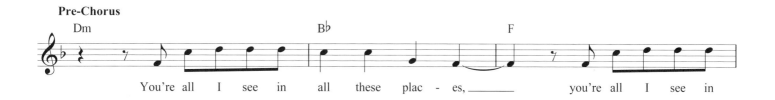
You're all I see in all these plac - es, _____ you're all I see in

all these fac - es. _____ So let's pre - tend we're run - ning out of time, _

Chorus

__ of time. ___ Ba - by, when they look up at _____ the sky, ___

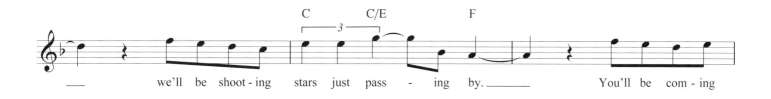
__ we'll be shoot - ing stars just pass - ing by. _____ You'll be com - ing

home with me ___ to - night _____ and we'll be burn - ing up like ne - on lights. __

__ Ba - by, when they look up at _____ the sky, _____ we'll be shoot - ing

stars just pass - ing by. _____ You'll be com - ing home with me _____ to - night _____

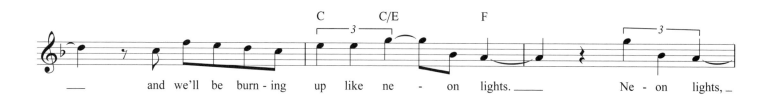

_____ and we'll be burn - ing up like ne - on lights. _____ Ne - on lights, _____

_____ ne - on lights, _____ ne - on lights. _____ Like ne - on lights. _____

_____ Oh, _____

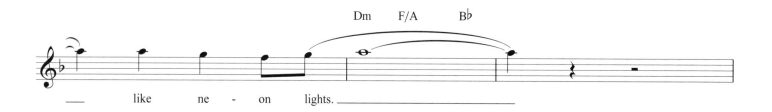

_____ like ne - on lights. _____

Verse
Half-time feel

Oh. _____ 3. Shin - ing like

stars 'cause we're beau - ti - ful. _____ (Beau - ti - ful.) _____

Pre-Chorus

You're all I see in all these plac - es, _____ you're all I see in

all these fac - es. _____ So let's pre-tend we're run - ning out of time, _

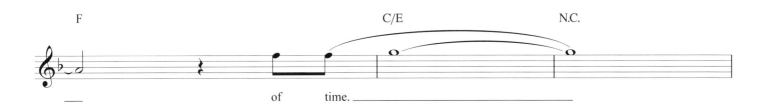

_ of time. _____

Outro-Chorus
End half-time feel

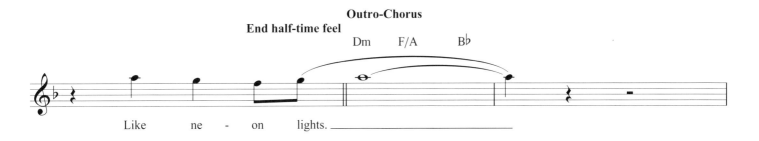

Like ne - on lights. _____

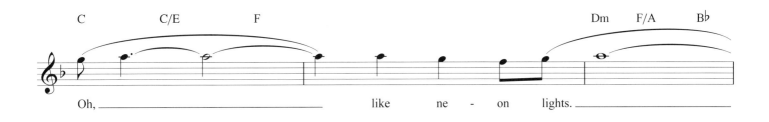

Oh, _____ like ne - on lights. _____

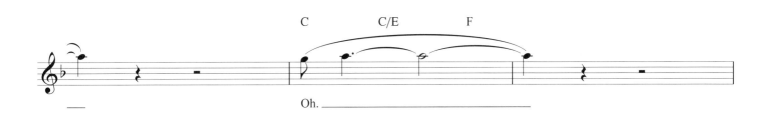

_ Oh. _____

Be still my heart 'cause it's freak - ing out.

Next to Me

Words and Music by Emeli Sandé, Harry Craze, Hugo Chegwin and Anup Paul

*Capo V

Strum Pattern: 1
Pick Pattern: 5

Intro
Moderately slow

*Optional: To match recording, place capo at 5th fret.

Verse

1. You won't find him drink-ing un-der ta - bles, roll-ing dice and stay-ing out till

mon-ey's spent and all my friends have van - ished, and I can't seem to find no help or love for

three. You won't ev-er find him be-ing un-faith - ful. You will find

free, I know there's no need for me to pan-ic, 'cause I'll find

__ him, you'll find __ him next to me.

__ him, I'll find __ him next to me. 2. You won't find him try'n' to chase the dev-

4. When the skies are grey and all the doors are clos-

- il for mon-ey, fame, for pow-er out of greed.

- ing, and the ris-ing pres-sure makes it hard to breathe, when all I

You won't nev-er find him where the rest __ go. You will find __ him, you'll find __ him next to

need's a hand to stop the tears from fall - ing, I will find __ him, I'll find __ him next to

Chorus

me.

me.

Next to me, __ oo, oo, __ next to me, __

Paradise

Words and Music by Guy Berryman, Jon Buckland, Will Champion, Chris Martin and Brian Eno

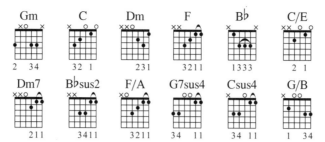

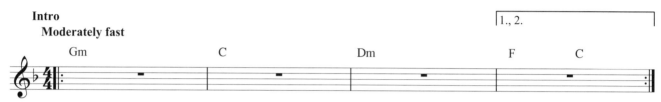

Strum Pattern: 3
Pick Pattern: 3

Verse

1. When she was just a girl, _____ she ex-pect-ed the world. _____

_____ But it flew a-way from her reach, _____ so she

ran a-way in her sleep _____ and dreamed of pa - ra, pa - ra, _____

Chorus

_____ pa-ra-dise, pa - ra, pa - ra, _____ pa-ra-dise, pa - ra, pa - ra, _____

_____ pa-ra-dise ev - 'ry-time she closed _____ her _____ eyes.

Interlude

* Oo, _____ oo. _____

*Lyrics sung 2nd time.

Verse

2. When she was just a girl, _____ she ex-pect-ed the world. _____

_____ But it flew a-way from her reach _____ and the

111

bul-lets catch in her teeth. _____ Life goes on, it gets ___ so heav-y, the

wheel ___ breaks the but - ter - fly. Ev - 'ry tear a wa - ter-fall. ___ In the

𝄋 Pre-Chorus

night, the storm - y night ___ she closed her ___ eyes. _____
- ing un - der - neath ___ the storm - y ___ skies _____

___ In the night, ___ the storm - y night, ___ a - way she'll ___
___ she said, "Oh, _____ I know this

Chorus

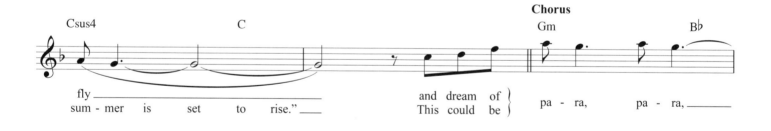

fly _____ and dream of } pa - ra, pa - ra, _____
sum - mer is set to rise." ___ This could be }

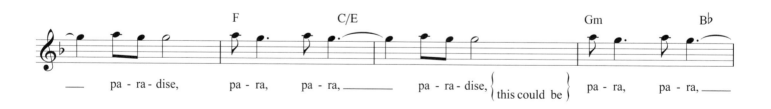

___ pa - ra - dise, pa - ra, pa - ra, _____ pa - ra - dise, { this could be } pa - ra, pa - ra, _____

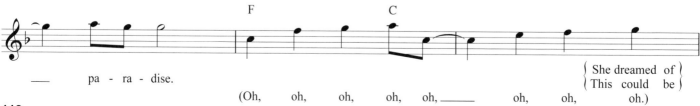

___ pa - ra - dise. { She dreamed of }
{ This could be }
(Oh, oh, oh, oh, oh, _____ oh, oh, oh.)

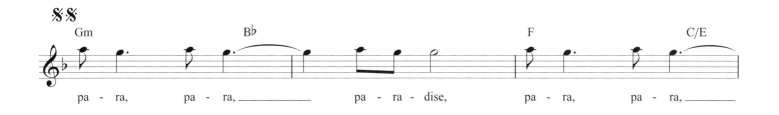

pa - ra, pa - ra, pa - ra - dise, pa - ra, pa - ra,

pa - ra - dise, {2., 3. could be} pa - ra, pa - ra, pa - ra - dise.

2nd time, To Coda 1 ⊕   *3rd time, To Coda 2* ⊕ **Bridge**

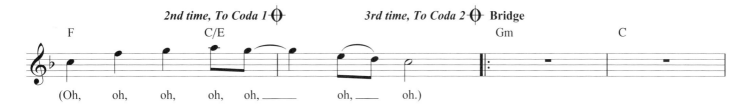

(Oh, oh, oh, oh, oh, oh, oh.)

La, la, la, la, la, la, la, la, la, la, la, la,

D.S. al Coda 1   ⊕ **Coda 1**

la, la la, la, la, la, la, la. And so ly -   oh, oh.)

Guitar Solo   1.   2.   *D.S.S. al Coda 2*

This could be

⊕ **Coda 2**
Outro

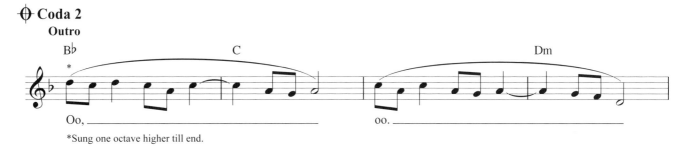

Oo,   oo.

*Sung one octave higher till end.

Oo,   oo.

Put Your Records On

Words and Music by John Beck, Steven Chrisanthou and Corinne Bailey Rae

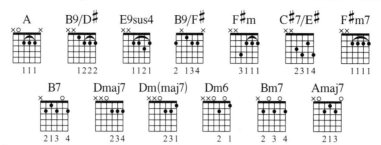

Strum Pattern: 1
Pick Pattern: 1

Intro
Moderately slow

Verse

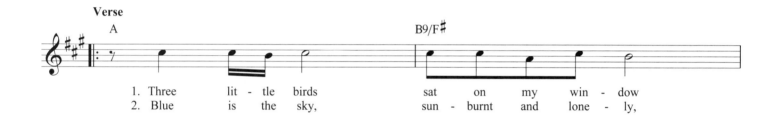

1. Three lit - tle birds sat on my win - dow
2. Blue is the sky, sun - burnt and lone - ly,

and they told me I don't need to wor - ry. _____
sip - pin' tea in a bar by the road - side. _____

Sum - mer came like cin - na - mon, so _____ sweet.
Don't you let those oth - er boys fool _____ you,

Lit - tle girls dou - ble dutch on the con - crete. _____
got - ta love that Af - ro hair - do. _____

Pre-Chorus

May - be some - times we _____ got it wrong but it's
May - be some - times we _____ feel a - fraid but it's

B7   Dmaj7

al - right.   The more ___ things seem ___ to change, ___   the more __
al - right.   The more ___ you stay ___ the same, ___   the more __

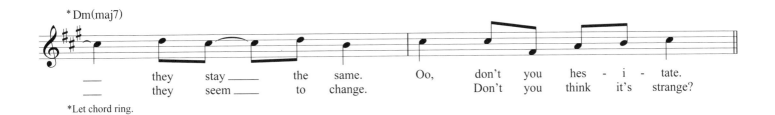

*Dm(maj7)

___ they stay ___ the same.   Oo, don't you hes - i - tate.
___ they seem ___ to change.   Don't you think it's strange?

*Let chord ring.

Chorus

A   B9/F♯   E9sus4

Girl, put your rec - ords on. ___ Tell me your fav -'rite song. _   You go a - head let your hair _

A   B9/F♯

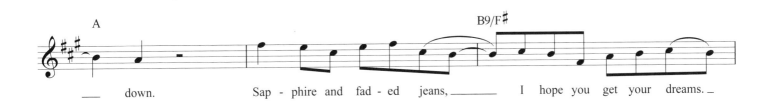

___ down.   Sap - phire and fad - ed jeans, ___   I hope you get your dreams. _

E9sus4   A   Dmaj7

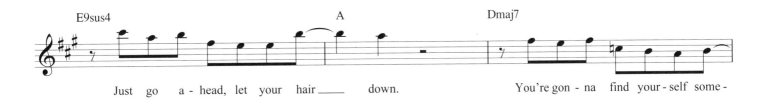

Just go a - head, let your hair ___ down.   You're gon - na find your - self some -

                          1.   2.

                                                  Bridge

Dm6   A   Bm7

- where,   some - how. ___   ___ 'Twas more than I could take,

                          F♯m

pit - y for pit - y's sake.   Some nights kept me a - wake,   I thought that I was strong - er. _

Bm7 ... Dmaj7 ... Bm7

When you gon-na re - al - ize   that you don't e - ven have to   try____ an - y long - er?

Chorus

*Dmaj7   A   N.C.

Do____ what you want   to.____   Girl, put your rec - ords on._____

*Let chord ring.

B9/F♯   E9sus4   A

____ Tell me your fav -'rite song.__   You go a - head, let your hair____ down.

B9/F♯   E9sus4

Sap - phire and fad - ed jeans,_____ I hope you get your dreams. _   Just go a - head, let your hair _

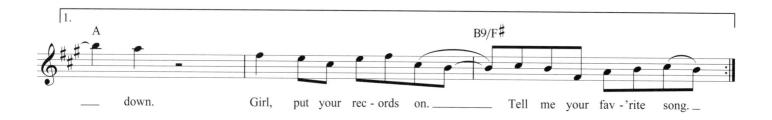

1.

A   B9/F♯

____ down.   Girl, put your rec - ords on._____ Tell me your fav -'rite song. _

2.

A   **Dmaj7

____ down.   Oo,_____ you're gon - na find your - self some -

**Let chords ring till end.

Dm(maj7)   Amaj7

- where,_____ some - how._____

Rhythm of Love

Words and Music by Tim Lopez

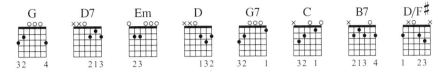

*Capo I

Strum Pattern: 3
Pick Pattern: 1

Intro
Moderately slow, in 2

*Optional: To match recording, place capo at 1st fret.

Verse

1. My head is stuck in the clouds. She begs me ___
2. Well, my heart beats like a drum, a gui - tar string ___

___ to come down, says, "Boy, quit fool - in' a - round." ___
___ to the strum, a beau - ti - ful song ___ to be ___ sung.

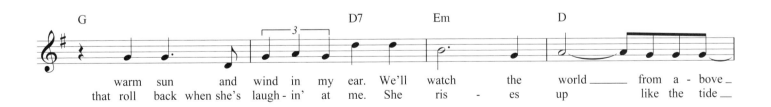

I told her, "I love the view ___ from up here,
She's got blue eyes deep ___ like the sea

warm sun and wind in my ear. We'll watch the world ___ from a - bove ___
that roll back when she's laugh - in' at me. She ris - es up like the tide ___

___ as it turns ___ to the rhy - thm of ___ love." }
___ the mo - ment her lips meet ___ mine. }

We may

% **Chorus**

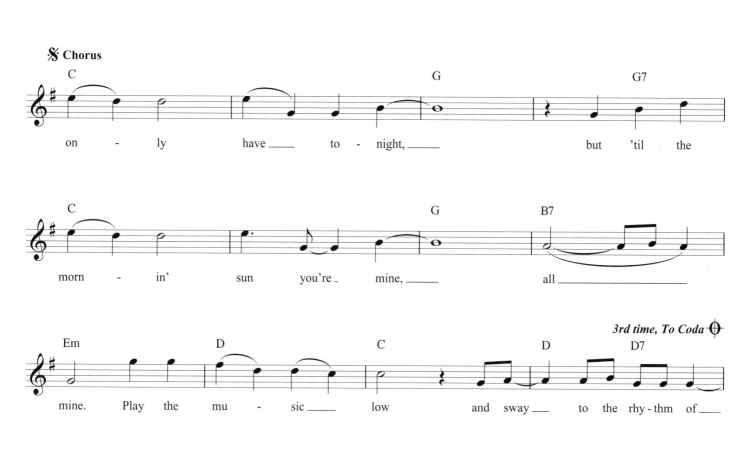

on - ly have ____ to - night, ____ but 'til the

morn - in' sun you're _ mine, ____ all _____

3rd time, To Coda ⊕

mine. Play the mu - sic ____ low and sway ___ to the rhy - thm of ___

1.

2.

___ love.

Bridge

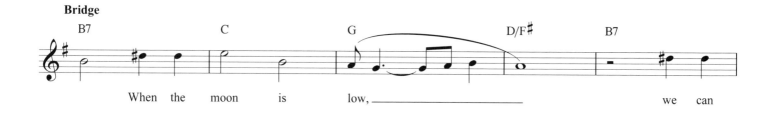

When the moon is low, _____ we can

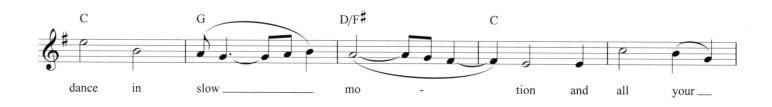

dance in slow _____ mo - tion and all your ___

tears will sub - side. All your tears _____ will ___

Interlude

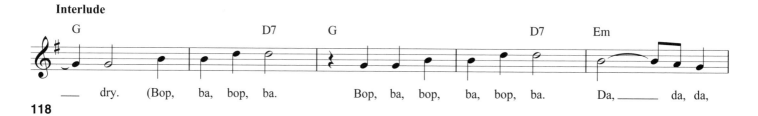

___ dry. (Bop, ba, bop, ba. Bop, ba, bop, ba, bop, ba. Da, _____ da, da,

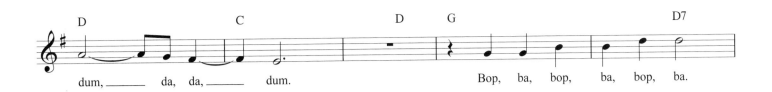

dum, _____ da, da, _____ dum. Bop, ba, bop, ba, bop, ba.

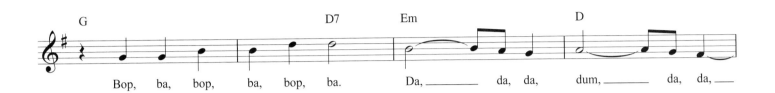

Bop, ba, bop, ba, bop, ba. Da, _____ da, da, dum, _____ da, da, _____

Verse

_____ dum.) 3. And long af - ter I've gone, you'll still be

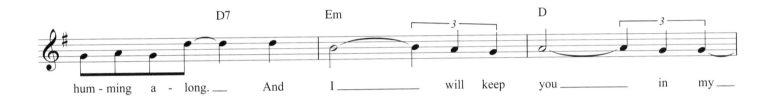

hum - ming a - long. _____ And I _____ will keep you _____ in my _____

D.S. al Coda

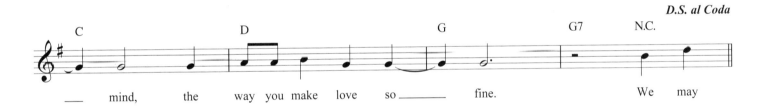

_____ mind, the way you make love so _____ fine. We may

⊕ Coda

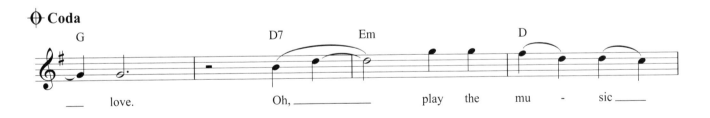

_____ love. Oh, _____ play the mu - sic _____

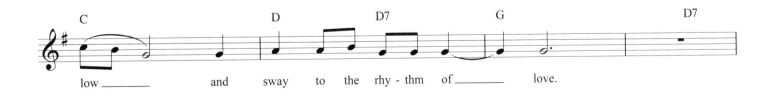

low _____ and sway to the rhy - thm of _____ love.

Yeah, sway to the rhy - thm of _____ love.

Radioactive

Words and Music by Daniel Reynolds, Benjamin McKee, Daniel Sermon, Alexander Grant and Josh Mosser

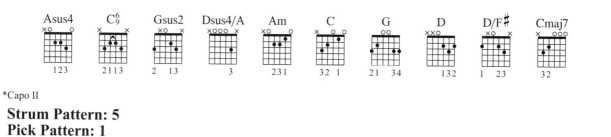

*Capo II

Strum Pattern: 5
Pick Pattern: 1

Intro
Slow

*Optional: To match recording, place capo at 2nd fret.

Verse

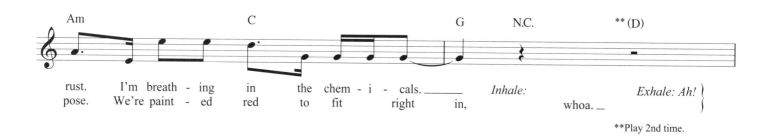

1. I'm wak - ing up to ash and dust, I wipe my brow and I sweat my
2. I raise my flag and dye my clothes. It's a rev-o-lu - tion I sup -

rust. I'm breath - ing in the chem - i - cals. ___ *Inhale:* *Exhale: Ah!*
pose. We're paint - ed red to fit right in, whoa. ___

**Play 2nd time.

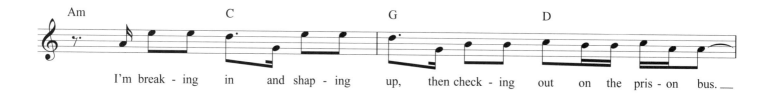

I'm break - ing in and shap - ing up, then check - ing out on the pris - on bus. ___

___ This is it, the a - poc - a - lypse, ___ whoa. ___ I'm wak - ing

𝄉 Pre-Chorus

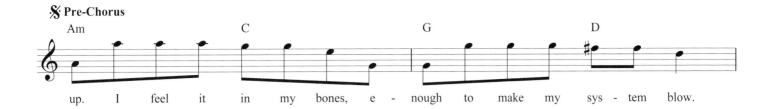

up. I feel it in my bones, e - nough to make my sys - tem blow.

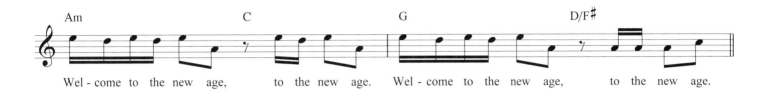

Wel - come to the new age, to the new age. Wel - come to the new age, to the new age.

Chorus

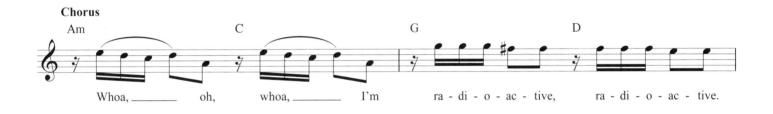

Whoa, _____ oh, whoa, _____ I'm ra - di - o - ac - tive, ra - di - o - ac - tive.

Fine

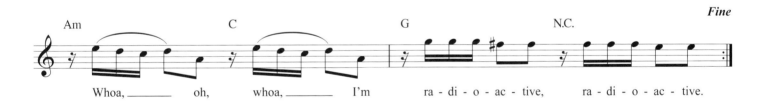

Whoa, _____ oh, whoa, _____ I'm ra - di - o - ac - tive, ra - di - o - ac - tive.

Bridge

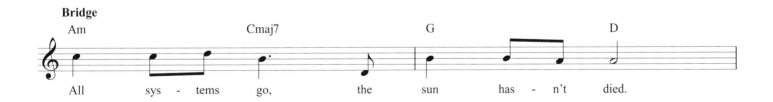

All sys - tems go, the sun has - n't died.

D.S. al Fine

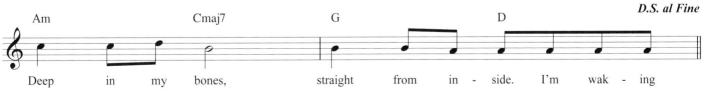

Deep in my bones, straight from in - side. I'm wak - ing

Royals

Words and Music by Ella Yelich-O'Connor and Joel Little

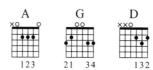

*Capo V

Strum Pattern: 6
Pick Pattern: 6

Verse

Moderately slow, in 2

N.C.(A)

1. I've nev-er seen a dia-mond in the flesh. ___
I, we've cracked the code. ___

*Optional: To match recording, place capo at 5th fret.

I cut my teeth on wed-ding rings ___ in the mov - ies. ___
We count our dol-lars on the train ___ to the par - ty. ___

And I'm not proud of my ad - dress ___
And ev - 'ry - one who knows us knows ___

in the torn - up town, no post-code en - vy. ___
that we're fine with this. We did-n't come from mon - ey. ___

Pre-Chorus

A

But ev-'ry song's_ like gold teeth, Grey Goose, trip-pin' in the bath-room, blood stains, ball gowns,

G   D

trash-in' the ho-tel room. We don't care, _ we're driv-in' Cad-il-lacs in our dreams. _

But ev-'ry-bod-y's like Cris - tal, May - bach, dia-monds on your time-piece,

jet planes, is - lands, ti - gers on a gold leash. We don't care, __

we aren't caught up in your love af - fair. __ And we'll nev - er be

Chorus

roy - als. (Roy - als.) It don't run in our __ blood. __ That kind of

lux just ain't __ for us. _____ We crave a dif - f'rent kind __ of buzz. __

3rd time, To Coda

__ Let me be __ your rul - er. (Rul - er.) You can call me queen __ bee, __

__ and, ba - by, I'll rule. (I'll rule, I'll rule, I'll rule.)

1.

Interlude

D   N.C.(A)

Let me live that fan - ta - sy.

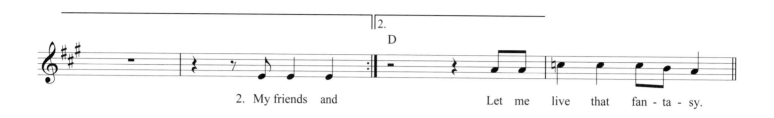

2.

D

2. My friends and   Let me live that fan - ta - sy.

Bridge

A

(Oh, _____   oh, _____   oh.) _____

G   D

_____ we're big - ger than we ev - er dreamed,   And I'm in love with

A

be - ing queen.   (Oh, _____   oh, _____   oh.) _____

G   D   N.C.

_____ life is great with - out a care. _____ We aren't caught up in your love af - fair. _____

D.S. al Coda   ⊕ **Coda**

D   N.C.

_____ And we'll nev - er be   Let me live that fan - ta - sy.

She Runs Away

Words and Music by Duncan Sheik

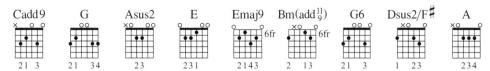

Strum Pattern: 1
Pick Pattern: 5

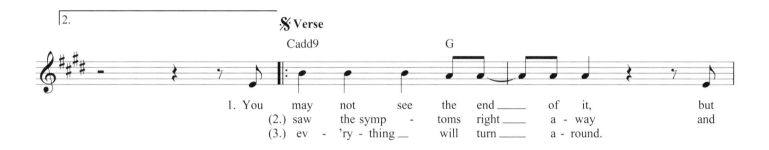

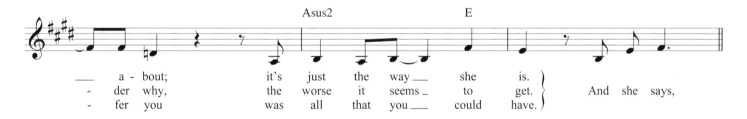

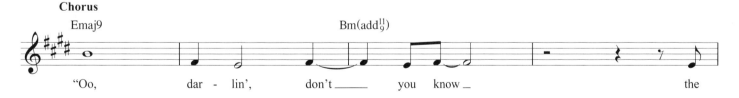

Emaj9   *Bm(add⁹¹¹)*

"Oo,   babe,   why   don't   you ____   let   her ____   go?

G6   *Dsus2/F#*   *Asus2*

Hap - pi - ness ___ ain't   nev - er   how ___ you   think ___ it   should _ be

1.   **Verse**

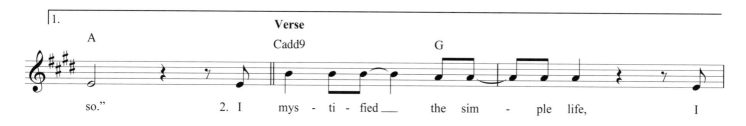

A   *Cadd9*   *G*

so."   2. I   mys - ti - fied ___ the   sim - ple life,   I

Asus2   *E*   *Cadd9*   *G*

cov - ered up ___ with con - scious - ness,   I   saw   my - self   and   broke _

2.

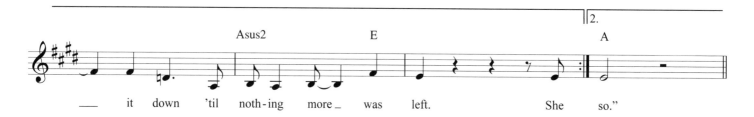

Asus2   *E*   *A*

___ it   down   'til   noth - ing   more _ was   left.   She   so."

Bridge

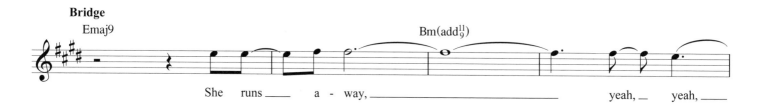

Emaj9   *Bm(add⁹¹¹)*

She   runs ___ a - way,   yeah, __ yeah, ___

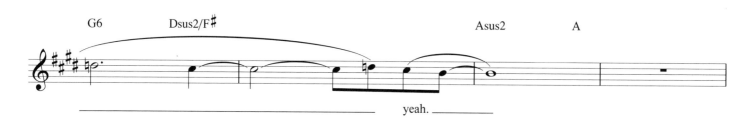

G6   *Dsus2/F#*   *Asus2*   *A*

yeah. ___

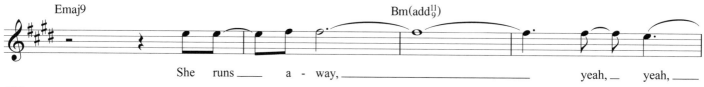

Emaj9   *Bm(add⁹¹¹)*

She   runs ___ a - way,   yeah, __ yeah, ___

Rude

Words and Music by Nasri Atweh, Mark Pellizzer, Alex Tanas, Ben Spivak and Adam Messinger

Say Something

Words and Music by Ian Axel, Chad Vaccarino and Mike Campbell

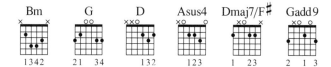

Strum Pattern: 8
Pick Pattern: 8

Intro
Slow, in 2

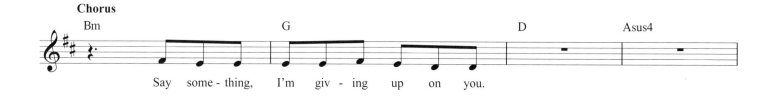

Chorus

Say some-thing, I'm giv-ing up on you.

I'll be the one if you want me to.

An - y - where I would have fol - lowed you.

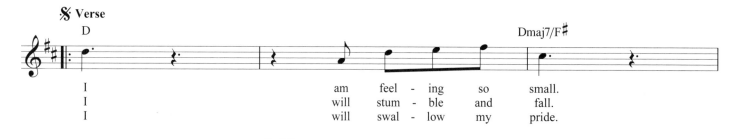

Say some-thing, I'm giv - ing up on you.

1. And

% Verse

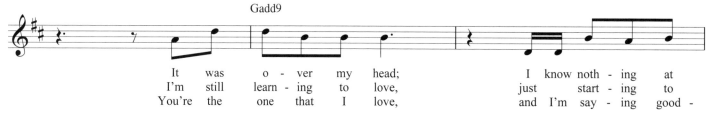

I am feel - ing so small.
I will stum - ble and fall.
I will swal - low my pride.

It was o - ver my head; I know noth - ing at
I'm still learn - ing to love, just start - ing to
You're the one that I love, and I'm say - ing good -

all.
crawl.
bye.

2. And

Chorus

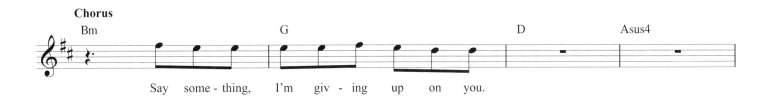

Say some-thing, I'm giv-ing up on you.

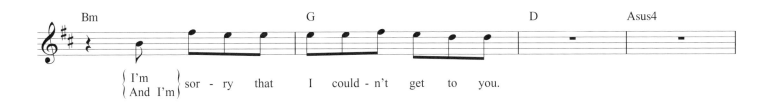

{ I'm }
{ And I'm } sor - ry that I could - n't get to you.

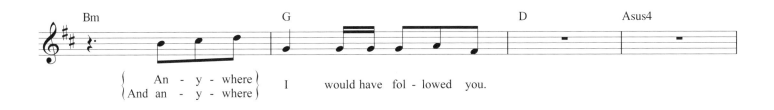

{ An - y - where }
{ And an - y - where } I would have fol - lowed you.

To Coda ✛

D.S. al Coda
(take 2nd ending)

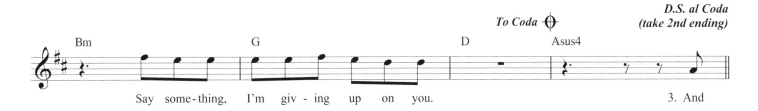

Say some-thing, I'm giv-ing up on you.

3. And

✛ **Coda**

Say some-thing, I'm giv-ing up on you.

Say some - thing.

Shooting Star

Words and Music by Adam Young, Mikkel Eriksen, Daniel Thomas Omelio,
Matthew Arnold Thiessen and Tor Erik Hermansen

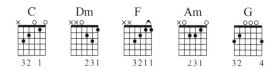

Strum Pattern: 1
Pick Pattern: 1

Intro
Moderately

Verse

1. Close your ti - red eyes, ____ re - lax and then ____ count from one to ten ____
2. Gaze in - to my eyes ____ when the fi - re starts, ____ and fan the flame so hot,

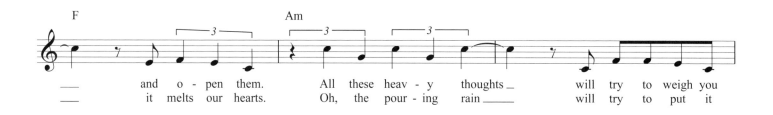

____ and o - pen them. All these heav - y thoughts ____ will try to weigh you
____ it melts our hearts. Oh, the pour - ing rain ____ will try to put it

down, but not this time. ____ Way up in the air, ____ you're fin - 'lly free, ____
out, but not this time. ____ Let your col - ors burn ____ and bright - ly burst ____

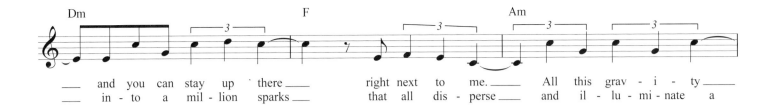

Dm   F   Am

__ and you can stay up there __ right next to me. __ All this grav-i-ty __
__ in-to a mil-lion sparks __ that all dis-perse __ and il-lu-mi-nate a

         Dm   F

__ will try to pull you down, but not this time. __   When the sun __
world that-'ll try to bring you down, but not this time. __

% **Chorus**

C   F

__ goes down and the lights __ burn out, then it's time __ for you __ to shine __

          Am

__ bright-er than a shoot - ing __ star; __ so shine no mat-ter

F   C

where you __ are. __ Fill the dark - est night with a bril -

          F

- liant light, 'cause it's time __ for you __ to shine __ bright-er than a

Am   F

shoot - ing __ star; __ so shine, no mat-ter where you __ are __

C

to - night. ____ Whoa, _____ whoa, _____

F

whoa. _____ Bright - er than a shoot - ing ____ star; ____

Am

3rd time, To Coda

F

1.

____ shine no mat - ter where you ____ are _____ to - night. __

2.

Bridge

G

C

F

____ to - night. ____ A thou - sand heart - beats beat in time __

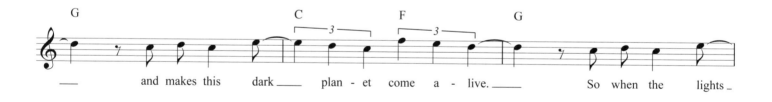

G

C

F

G

3

3

____ and makes this dark ____ plan - et come a - live. ____ So when the lights __

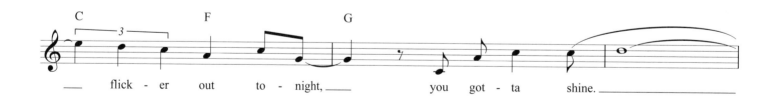

C

F

G

3

____ flick - er out to - night, ____ you got - ta shine. _____

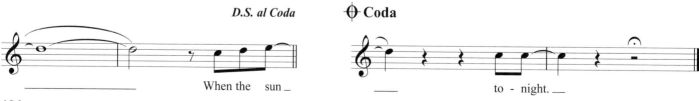

D.S. al Coda

Coda

____ When the sun __ ____ to - night. ____

Skinny Love

Words and Music by Justin Vernon

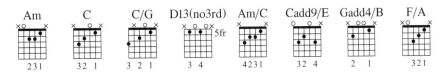

Strum Pattern: 5
Pick Pattern: 1

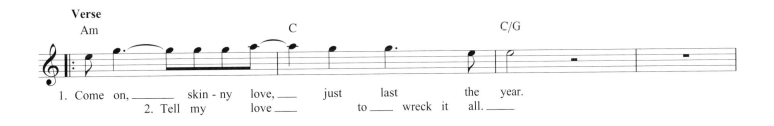

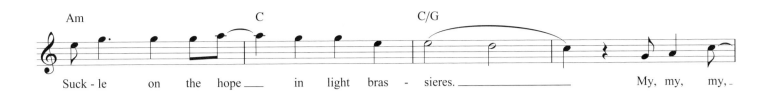

Am | C | C/G

Suck - le   on   the   hope ____ in   light   bras - sieres. _____ My,   my,   my, _

Am | C | C/G

__   my,   my,   my, ____ my, __ my.   Sul - len   load   is

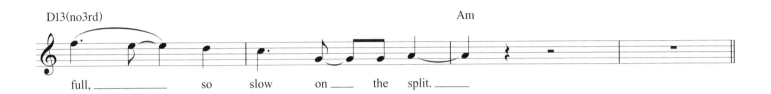

D13(no3rd) | Am

full, _____ so   slow   on ____ the   split. ____

Interlude   *D.S. al Coda*

Am/C | C

And   I've

⊕ **Coda**

Cadd9/E | Gadd4/B | F/A

Who will   love   you?   Who will   fight? _____

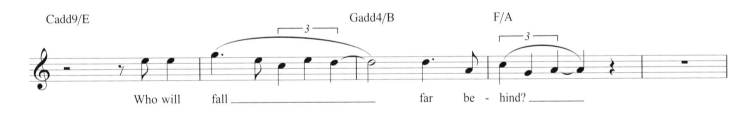

Cadd9/E | 3 | Gadd4/B | F/A | 3

Who will   fall _____ far   be - hind? _____

Outro

Am | C | C/G   *Play 3 times*

D13(no3rd) | Am | C

Skyfall

from the Motion Picture SKYFALL

Words and Music by Adele Adkins and Paul Epworth

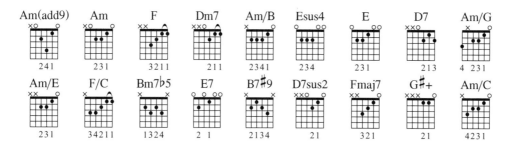

*Capo III

Strum Pattern: 3
Pick Pattern: 3

Intro
Slow

*Optional: To match recording, place capo at 3rd fret.

1. This is the end. ___

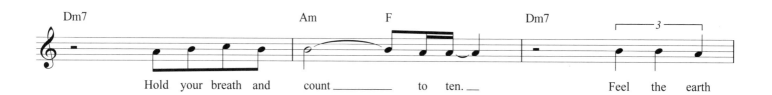

Hold your breath and count ___ to ten. ___ Feel the earth

move and then ___ hear my heart burst a -

gain. 2. For this is the end. ___ I've drowned and dreamt ___ this
where we start, ___ a thou - sand miles ___ and

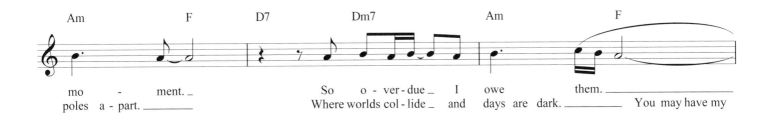

Am   F   D7   Dm7   Am   F

mo - ment. _ So o - ver-due _ I owe them. _

poles a - part. _____ Where worlds col - lide _ and days are dark. _____ You may have my

D7   Dm7   Am/B   Esus4   E

_ Swept a - way, _ I'm stol - en.

num - ber, you can take my name _____ but you'll nev-er have _ my heart. _____ Let the

𝄋 Chorus

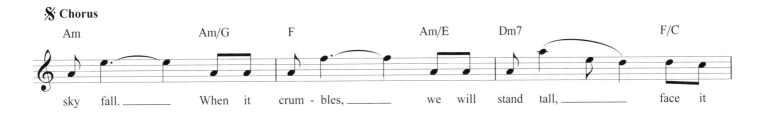

Am   Am/G   F   Am/E   Dm7   F/C

sky fall. _____ When it crum - bles, _____ we will stand tall, _____ face it

Bm7♭5   E7   Am   Am/G   F   Am/E

all to - geth - er. Let the sky fall. _____ When it crum - bles, _____ we will

3rd time, To Coda ⊕ |1.

D7   B7♯9   E7   Am   F

stand tall, _____ face it all to - geth - er at sky - fall.

D7   Dm7   Am   F   D7   Dm7

At sky - fall.   3. Sky - fall is

|2.

Interlude

Am

fall. (Let the sky fall. When it crum - bles, we will stand tall.

Let the sky fall. When it crum - bles,

Bridge

D7sus2

we will stand tall.) Where you _ go, I go. What you see,

Fmaj7   Am/G   G#+   3   Am   Am/G

I see. I know I'll nev - er be me _ with - out the se - cu - ri - ty _ of your

Fmaj7   Am/E   Dm7   Am/C   Am/B   Esus4 E   *D.S. al Coda*

lov - ing arms keep - ing me from harm. Put your hand in my hand and we'll stand. _ Let the

Coda

Am   Am/G   F   Am/E   Dm7   F/C

fall. Let the sky fall. _____ We will stand tall _____

Freely

Bm7♭5   E7   Am   Am/G   F   Am/E D7sus2

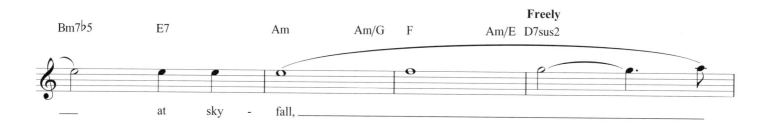

_ at sky - fall, _____

E   Am(add9)

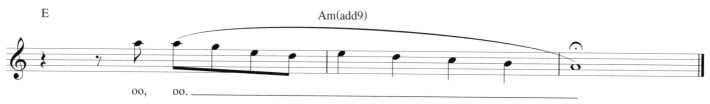

oo, oo. _____

Someone Like You

Words and Music by Adele Adkins and Dan Wilson

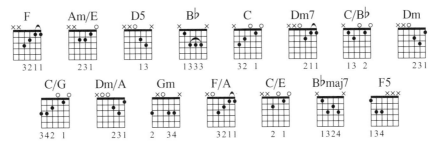

*Capo IV

Strum Pattern: 3
Pick Pattern: 3

Intro
Slow

*Optional: To match recording, place capo at 4th fret.
**Use Pattern 10 for 2/4 meas.

Verse

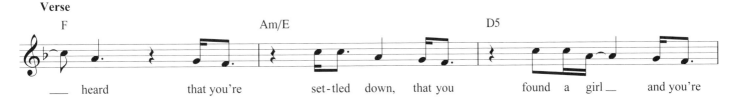

___ heard that you're set-tled down, that you found a girl ___ and you're

mar-ried now. ___ I heard that your dreams came true, guess she

gave you things ___ I did-n't give to you. ___ Old ___ friend, why are you so ___

___ shy? ___ Ain't like you to hold ___ back or ___ hide ___ from the light. ___ I

Pre-Chorus

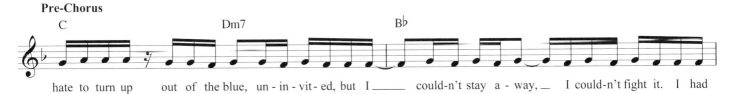

hate to turn up out of the blue, un-in-vit-ed, but I ___ could-n't stay a-way, ___ I could-n't fight it. I had

hoped you'd see my face and that you'd be re-mind-ed that for me it is-n't o - ver. ____

𝄋 **Chorus**

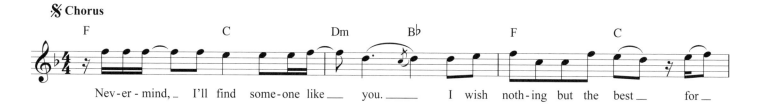

Nev-er - mind, _ I'll find some-one like ___ you. _____ I wish noth-ing but the best _ for _

2nd time, To Coda 1 ⊕

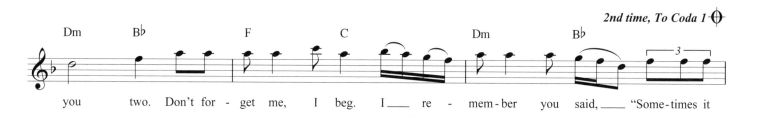

you two. Don't for - get me, I beg. I _ re - mem-ber you said, ___ "Some-times it

lasts in love, but some - times it hurts in - stead." _____ Some - times it

To Coda 2 ⊕

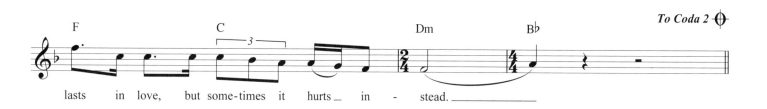

lasts in love, but some-times it hurts _ in - stead. _____

Verse

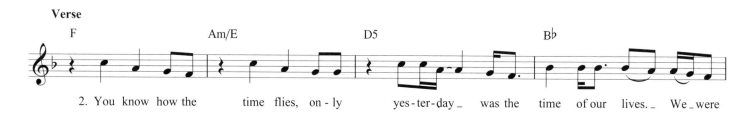

2. You know how the time flies, on - ly yes-ter-day _ was the time of our lives. _ We _ were

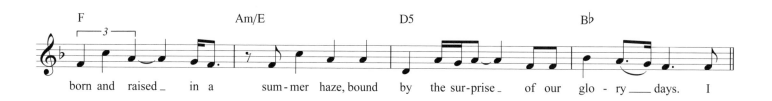

born and raised _ in a sum-mer haze, bound by the sur-prise _ of our glo - ry ___ days. I

Pre-Chorus

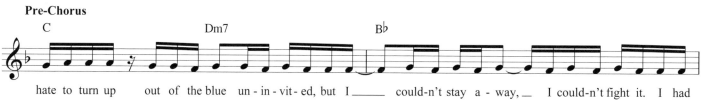

hate to turn up out of the blue un - in - vit-ed, but I _____ could-n't stay a - way, _ I could-n't fight it. I had

hoped you'd see my face and that you'd be re-mind-ed that for me it is-n't o - ver. _____

Coda 1

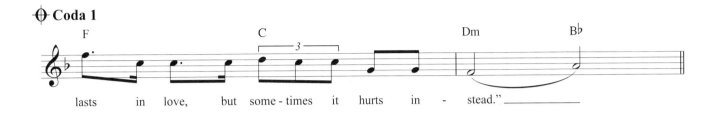

lasts in love, but some - times it hurts in - stead." _____

Bridge

Noth - ing com - pares, no wor - ries or cares, re - grets and mis - takes, they're mem - o - ries made.

Who would have known how _____ bit - ter - sweet _____ this would taste?

Chorus

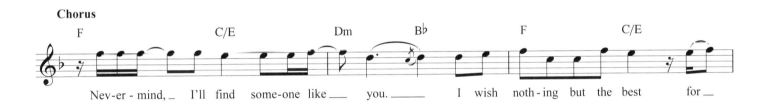

Nev - er - mind, _ I'll find some-one like _____ you. _____ I wish noth - ing but the best for _____

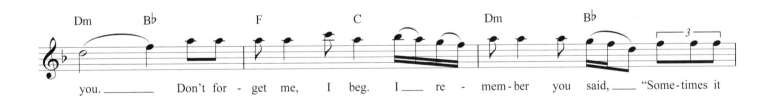

you. _____ Don't for - get me, I beg. I _____ re - mem - ber you said, _____ "Some - times it

D.S. al Coda 2

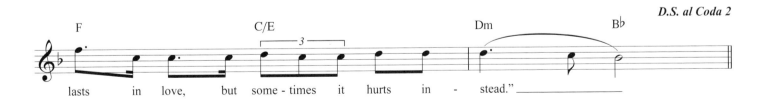

lasts in love, but some - times it hurts in - stead." _____

Coda 2

Stay

Words and Music by Mikky Ekko and Justin Parker

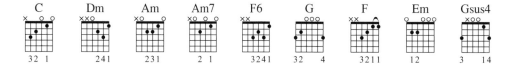

Strum Pattern: 4
Pick Pattern: 1

Intro
Moderately

Verse

Female:
1. All a-long __ it was a fe - ver. A cold __

__ sweat, hot - head - ed be - liev - er. I threw my

hands in the air, __ said, "Show me some - thin'." __

Male: 2. It's not much of a life you're liv - in'.

He said, "If you dare, __ come a lit - tle clos - er."

It's not __ just some - thin' you take; it's giv - en.

Pre-Chorus

'Round and a-round and a-round and a-round we go. __

__ Oh, __ now, tell me now, tell me now, tell me now you know. __

Chorus

__ Not real-ly sure how to feel a-bout __ it. Some-

- thin' in the way you move __ makes __ me feel like I can't __

live with-out __ you. {Well, / Yeah,} it __ takes me all the way. __ I want you to stay. __

Bridge

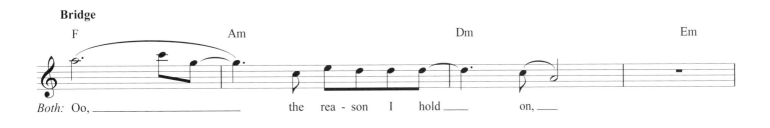

Both: Oo, _____ the rea-son I hold __ on, __

oo, _____ 'cause I need this hole gone. __

Fun - ny you're the bro - ken one but I'm the on - ly one who need - ed sav - in'.

'Cause when you nev - er see the light, it's hard to know which one of us is

Chorus

cav - in'. *Female:* Not real - ly sure how to feel a - bout __ it. Some-

- thin' in the way you move __ *Both:* makes __ me feel like I can't __

live with - out __ you. Well, it _____ takes me all __ the way. __ *Female:* I want you to stay. __

Outro

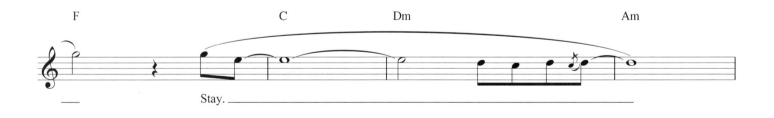

__ Stay. _____

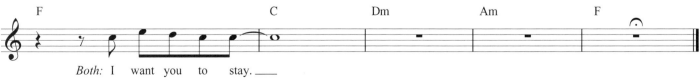

Both: I want you to stay. ____

146

Stereo Hearts

Words and Music by Travis McCoy, Adam Levine, Brandon Lowry, Daniel Omelio, Benjamin Levin and Ammar Malik

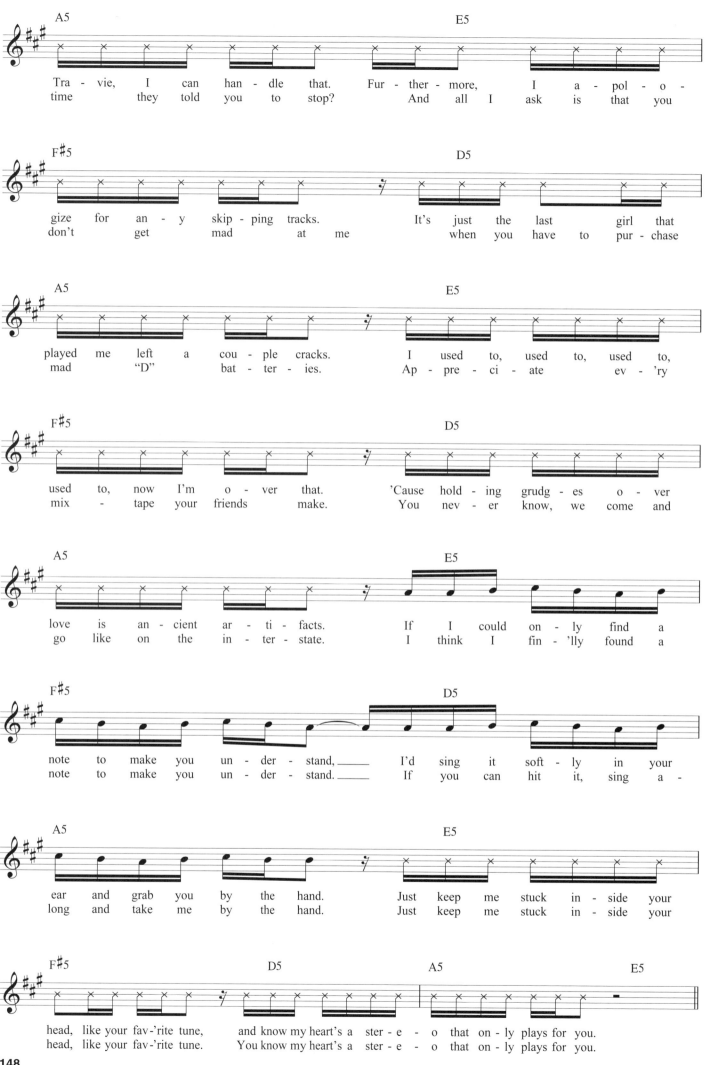

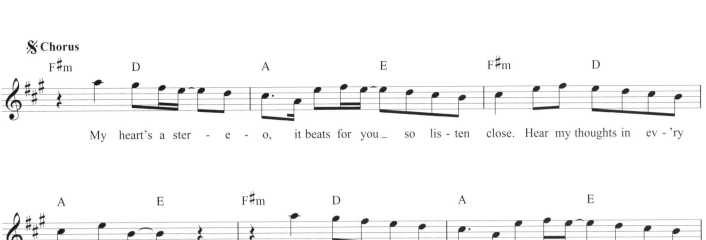

% Chorus

My heart's a ster - e - o, it beats for you __ so lis - ten close. Hear my thoughts in ev - 'ry

no - o - ote. __ Make me your ra - di - o, and turn me up __ when you feel

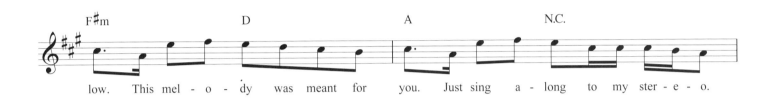

low. This mel - o - dy was meant for you. Just sing a - long to my ster - e - o.

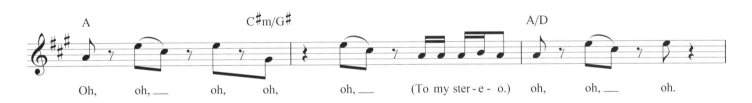

Oh, oh, __ oh, oh, oh, __ (To my ster - e - o.) oh, oh, __ oh.

3rd time, To Coda ⊕ | 1.

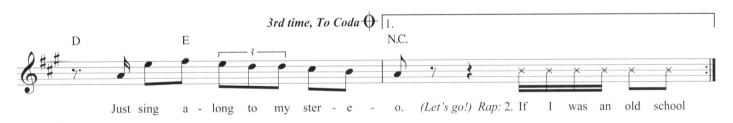

Just sing a - long to my ster - e - o. *(Let's go!) Rap:* 2. If I was an old school

| 2.

Bridge

o. I on - ly pray you'll nev - er leave me be - hind, __ *(Never leave me.)* be - cause good mu - sic can be

so hard to find. __ *(So hard to find.)* I'll take your head and hold it clos - er to mine. __ *(Yeah.)*

D.S. al Coda   ⊕ **Coda**

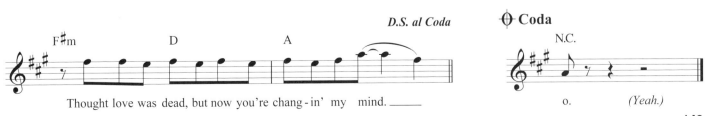

Thought love was dead, but now you're chang - in' my mind. _____   o. *(Yeah.)*

Stay with Me

Words and Music by Sam Smith, James Napier and William Edward Phillips

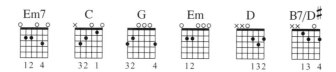

*Capo V

Strum Pattern: 3
Pick Pattern: 3

Intro
Moderately slow

*Optional: To match recording, place capo at 5th fret.

Verse

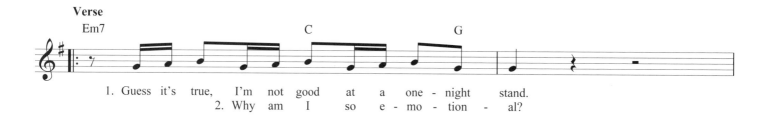

1. Guess it's true, I'm not good at a one-night stand.
2. Why am I so e-mo-tion-al?

But I still need love 'cause I'm just a man.
No, it's not a good look. Gain some self-con-trol.

These nights nev-er seem to go to plan.
And deep down I know this nev-er works.

I don't want you to leave, will you hold my hand?
But you can lay with me so it does-n't hurt.

Oh, won't you

Chorus

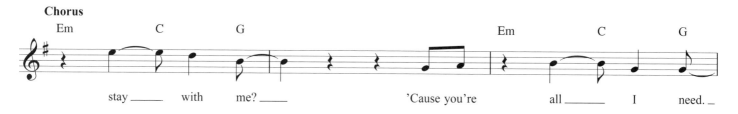

stay with me? 'Cause you're all I need.

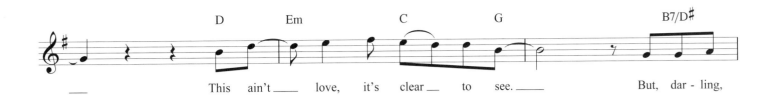

This ain't ____ love, it's clear __ to see. ____ But, dar - ling,

stay ____ with me. ____   Oh, _____

Bridge

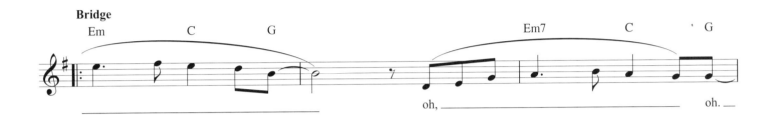

oh, _____ oh. __

Outro-Chorus

Oh, _____ __   Oh, won't you stay ____ with me? __

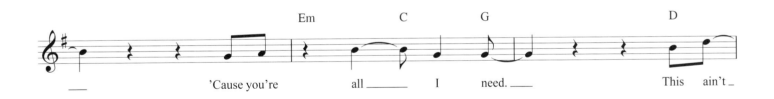

'Cause you're all ____ I need. ____ This ain't __

love, it's clear __ to see. ____ But, dar - ling, stay ____ with me. __

Oh, won't you __

Steal My Kisses

Words and Music by Ben Harper

Strum Pattern: 5
Pick Pattern: 1

Intro
Moderately, in 2

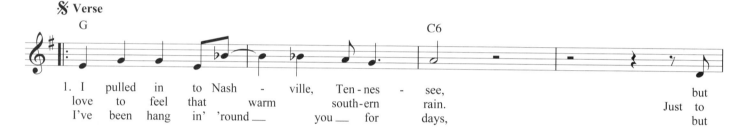

1. I pulled in to Nash - ville, Ten - nes - see, but
love to feel that warm south - ern rain. Just to
I've been hang in' 'round ___ you ___ for days, but

you would - n't e - ven come ___ a - round ___ to see me. ___ And
hear it fall ___ is the sweet - est sound ___ ing thing. And to
when I lean in, you just turn your head a - way. ___ Whoa, ___

since you're head - ing up ___ to Car - o - li - na, you
see it fall on your sim - ple coun - try dress, it's like ___
___ no, ___ you did - n't mean ___ that. She said, "I

3rd time, To Coda 1 ⊕

know I'm gon - na be right ___ there be - hind ___ ya. }
___ heav - en to me, ___ I must con - fess. ___ }
love the way you think but I hate the way you act." ___ }

'Cause I

Chorus

{ 1., 2. al - ways }
{   3. Al - ways } have ___ to steal my kiss - es from you.

I

Stuck Like Glue

Words and Music by Kristian Bush, Shy Carter, Kevin Griffin and Jennifer Nettles

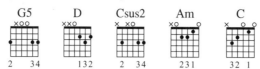

*Capo VI

Strum Pattern: 6
Pick Pattern: 6

Intro
Fast

*Optional: To match recording, place capo at 6th fret.

Verse

1. Ab - so - lute - ly no one that knows me _____ bet - ter,
2. *See additional lyrics*

no _____ one that can make me feel so _____ good.

How _ did we stay so long to - geth - er when ev - 'ry - bod - y,

ev - 'ry - bod - y said we nev - er would? _ And just when

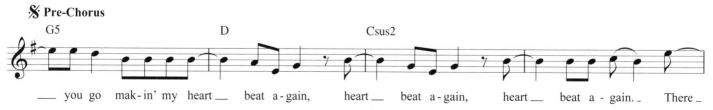

I, I start to think _ they're right, that love has died, _ there _

Pre-Chorus

_ you go mak - in' my heart _ beat a - gain, heart _ beat a - gain, heart _ beat a - gain. _ There _

154

you go makin' me feel ___ like a kid. Won't you do it, 'n' do it one time? There ___

you go pull-in' me right ___ back in, ___ right ___ back in, ___ right ___ back in, and I

know _____ I'm nev-er let-tin' this go. _____ I'm stuck on

Chorus

you. Wuh oh, ___ wuh oh, stuck like glue. You and me, ba-by, we're stuck like glue. ___

3rd time, To Coda ⊕

Wuh oh, ___ wuh oh, stuck like glue. You and me, ba-by, we're stuck like glue. ___

Bridge

Wuh oh, ___ wuh oh, you al-most stay out, too stuck to-geth-er from the A - T - L. ___

Wuh oh, ___ wuh oh, feel-in' kind-a sick. Just a spoon-ful o' sug-ar make it bet-ter real quick. I say,

wuh oh, ___ wuh oh, what ya gon-na do with that? Wuh oh, ___ wuh oh, come on o-ver here with that

Summertime Sadness

Words and Music by Elizabeth Grant and Rick Nowels

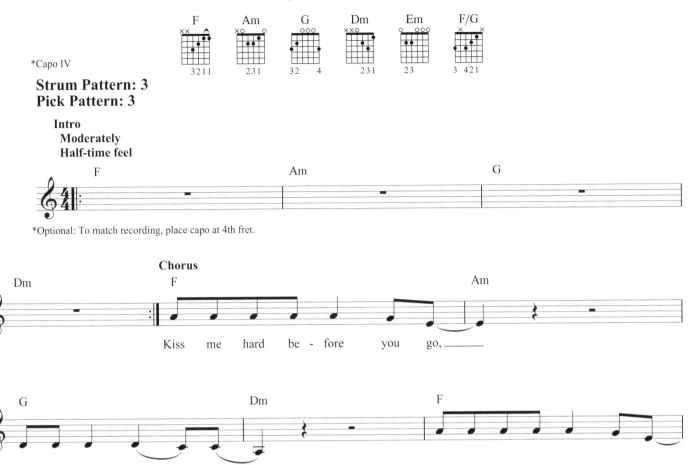

*Capo IV

Strum Pattern: 3
Pick Pattern: 3

Intro
Moderately
Half-time feel

*Optional: To match recording, place capo at 4th fret.

Chorus

Kiss me hard be - fore you go,

sum - mer - time sad - ness. ___ I just want - ed you to know ___ that, ba - by, you're ___ the best. ___ 1. I got my

Verse

red dress on to - night, ___ danc - in' in the dark ___ in the pale moon - light.
e - lec - tric to - night, ___ cruis - in' down the coast, ___ go - in' 'bout nine - ty - nine. ___

Done my hair up real big, beau - ty queen style. ___ High heels off.
Got my bad ___ ba - by by my heav - en - ly side. ___ I know if I go, ___

Pre-Chorus

I'm feel - in' a - live. ___ Oh, ___ my God, ___ I
I'll die hap - py to - night. ___

feel it in the air. Tel - e - phone wires _ a - bove _ are siz - zlin' like a snare. Hon - ey,

I'm _ on fire, _ I feel it ev - 'ry - where. Noth - in' scares me an - y - more. _

% Chorus

_ (Two, three, four.) Kiss me hard be - fore you go, _

sum - mer - time sad - ness. _ I just want - ed you to know _

End half-time feel

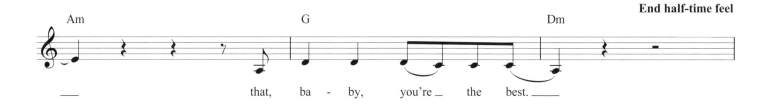

_ that, ba - by, you're _ the best. _

I got that sum - mer - time, sum - mer - time sad - ness. Su - su - sum - mer - time,

sum - mer - time sad - ness. Got that sum - mer - time, sum - mer - time sad - ness.

3rd time, To Coda ⊕

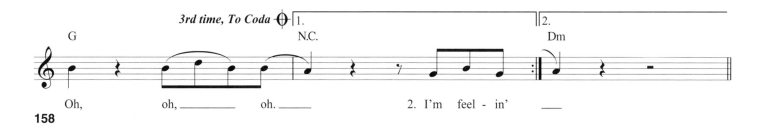

Oh, oh, _ oh. _ 2. I'm feel - in' _

Bridge
Half-time feel

Think I'll miss you for - ev - er like the stars miss the sun in the morn - ing sky.

Lat - er's bet - ter than nev - er. E - ven if you're gone, I'm gon - na

drive, (Drive.) drive.

Chorus

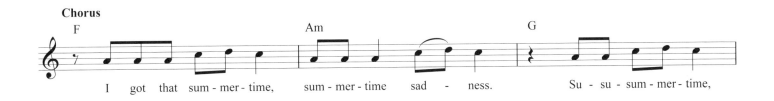

I got that sum - mer - time, sum - mer - time sad - ness. Su - su - sum - mer - time,

sum - mer - time sad - ness. Got that sum - mer - time, sum - mer - time sad - ness.

D.S. al Coda   ⊕ **Coda**

Oh, oh, oh.

Outro
Half-time feel

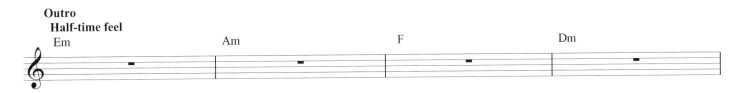

Teardrops on My Guitar

Words and Music by Taylor Swift and Liz Rose

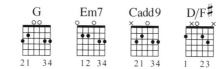

*Capo III

Strum Pattern: 3
Pick Pattern: 2

Intro
Moderately

*Optional: To match recording, place capo at 3rd fret.

Verse

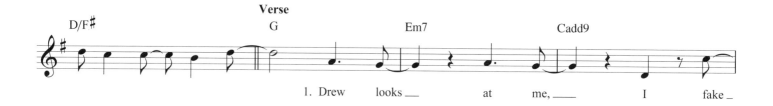

1. Drew looks ___ at me, ___ I fake ___

___ a smile so he won't see ___ that I want ___ and I'm need - in' ___ ev -

- 'ry - thing that we should be. ___ I'll bet she's beau - ti - ful, that girl he talks a - bout.

Verse

And she's got ev - 'ry-thing that I have to live with-out.

2. Drew talks ___ to me, ___
3. Drew walks ___ by me, ___

___ I laugh ___ 'cause it's so damn fun - ny ___ that I can't ___
___ can ___ he tell that I can't breathe? ___ And there he goes, ___

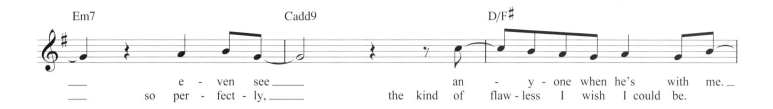

Em7   Cadd9   D/F#

__ e - ven see _____ an - y - one when he's with me. _

__ so per - fect - ly, _____ the kind of flaw - less I wish I could be.

Em7   Cadd9   G

__ He says he's so in love,   he's fi - n'lly got it right.   I won - der if he knows he's

She bet - ter hold him tight,   give him all her love,   look in those beau - ti - ful eyes _

Chorus

D/F#   G   D/F#

all I think a - bout at night.   He's } the rea - son for the tear - drops on my gui - tar,

__ and know she's luck - y 'cause he's }

Em7   Cadd9   G

the on - ly thing that keeps me wish - in' on a wish - in' star.   He's the song   in the car

D/F#   Em7   Cadd9

I keep sing - in'. Don't know why _____ I _____ do.

Interlude

G   Em7   Cadd9

D/F#   G   Em7   Cadd9   D/F#

Pre-Chorus

So, I drive home a - lone. As I turn out the light, I'll put his pic - ture down and

Chorus

may - be get some sleep to - night. 'Cause he's the rea - son for the tear - drops on my gui - tar,

the on - ly one who's got e - nough of me to break my heart. ___ He's the song in the car

I keep sing - in'. Don't know why ___ I ___ do. He's the time

tak - en up, but there's nev - er e - nough ___ and he's all ___ that I need to fall in -

Outro

- to. ___ Drew looks ___ at me, ___

___ I fake ___ a smile, so he won't see. ___

162

Toes

Words and Music by Shawn Mullins, Zac Brown, Wyatt Durrette and John Driskell Hopkins

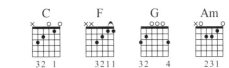

*Tune down 1/2 step:
(low to high) Eb-Ab-Db-Gb-Bb-Eb

Strum Pattern: 5
Pick Pattern: 1

Intro
Moderately fast

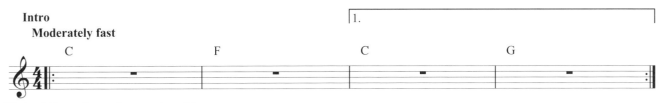

*Optional: To match recording, tune down 1/2 step.

I got my toes in the wa - ter, ass ___

___ in the sand, ___ not a wor - ry in the world, a cold beer in my hand. Life is good ___

___ to - day, life is good ___ to - day. 1. Well the

Verse

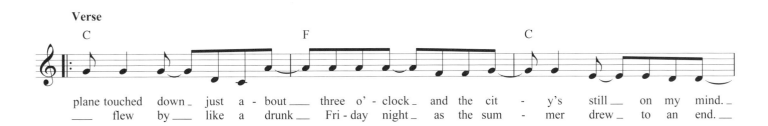

plane touched down ___ just a - bout ___ three o' - clock ___ and the cit - y's still ___ on my mind.
___ flew by ___ like a drunk ___ Fri - day night ___ as the sum - mer drew ___ to an end. ___

___ Bi - ki - nis and palm ___ trees danced ___ in my head, ___ I was still ___
They ___ can't be - lieve ___ that I just ___ could - n't leave and I bid ___

in the bag - gage line. ___ Con - crete and cars ___ are their own ___
a - dieu ___ to my friends. ___ 'Cause my ___ bar - ten - der, ___ she's ___

pri - son bars ___ like this ___ life I'm ___ liv - in' in. ___ But the
from the is - lands, her bod - y's been kissed ___ by the sun. ___ And

plane brought me far - ther, I'm sur - round - ed by wa - ter and I'm ___ not goin' back a - gain. ___
co - co - nut re - plac - es the smell ___ of the bar, ___ and I don't ___ know if it's her ___ or the rum. ___

Refrain

I got my toes in the wa - ter, ass ___ in the sand, ___ not a

wor - ry in the world, a cold beer in my hand. ___ Life is good ___ to - day,

life is good ___ to - day. A - di - os and va - ya con

𝄋 **Chorus**

Di - os,

yeah, I'm leav - in' G A. ___
a long way ___ from G A. ___
go - in' home ___ now to stay. ___

And if it weren't ___ for te - qui - la and pret - ty se - ño - ri - tas,
Yes, and all the mu - cha - chas, they call me "Big Pa - pa"
The se - ño - ri - tas don't care - o when there's no di - ne - ro.

164

I'd have no rea - son to stay.
when I throw pe - sos their way.
I got no mon - ey to stay.

A - di - os and va - ya con

3rd time, To Coda

Di - os,

yeah, I'm leav - in' G A.
a long way from G A.
go - in' home now to stay.

Gon - na lay in the hot sun and roll a big fat one and, and grab my gui - tar and
Some - one do me a fa - vor and pour me some Jä - ger and I'll grab my gui - tar and

*2nd time, let chord ring.

Interlude

play.
play.

1.   2.

D.S. al Coda

2. The four days

A - di - os and va - ya con

Coda

Outro-Refrain

Spoken: Just gonna drive up by the lake and put my ass in a lawn chair, toes

*Let chords ring, next 8 meas.

in the clay, not a wor - ry in the world, a P B R on the way. Life is good

to - day, life is good to - day.

165

Thinkin' 'Bout You

Words and Music by Frank Ocean and Shea Taylor

Strum Pattern: 3
Pick Pattern: 5

Intro
Slow, in 2

N.C.

1. A tor-

Verse

na - do flew a - round my room be - fore you came, ex - cuse the mess it made. It u -
like you, I just thought you were cool e - nough to kick it, got a beach house I could sell you in I -

- s'lly does - n't rain in South - ern Cal - i - for - nia, much like Ar - i - zo - na. My
- da - ho. Since you think I don't love you, I just thought you were cute, that's why I kissed you. Got a

eyes don't shed tears, but boy, they bawl when I'm
fight - er jet; I don't get to fly it though. I'm ly - ing down think - ing 'bout you, hoo,

no, no, no. I been think - ing 'bout you, you know, know, know. I been think - ing 'bout you, do you

think a - bout me still? Do you, do you? Or do you not

*Sung one octave higher throughout Chorus.

𝄋 Chorus

think so far a - head? 'Cause I been think - ing 'bout for -

*Sung one octave higher throughout Chorus.

Titanium

Words and Music by David Guetta, Sia Furler, Giorgio Tuinfort and Nik Van De Wall

*Capo III

Strum Pattern: 1
Pick Pattern: 1

Intro
Moderately

*Optional: To match recording, place capo at 3rd fret.

Verse

1. You shout it out, _____ but I _____ can't hear a word you say.
2. Cut me down, _____ but it's you _____ who have fur-ther to fall.

I'm talk-ing loud, _____ not say-ing much. _____
Mm, ghost town _____ and haunt-ed love. _____

I'm crit-i-cized, _____ but all _____ your bul-lets ric-o-chet.
Raise your voice; _____ sticks _____ and stones may break my bones.

You shoot me down, _____ but I get up. _____
Talk-ing loud, _____ not say-ing much. _____

Chorus

I'm bul-let-proof, _____ noth-ing to lose; _____ fire a-way, _____ fire _____ a-way. _____

_____ Ric-o-chet, _____ you take your aim; _____ fire a-way, _____ fire _____ a-way. _____

_____ You shoot me down, _____ but I won't fall; _____ I am ti-ta-ni-

Torn

Words and Music by Phil Thornalley, Scott Cutler and Anne Previn

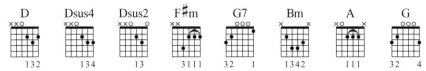

*Capo III

Strum Pattern: 2
Pick Pattern: 4

Intro
Moderately slow, in 2

*Optional: To match recording, place capo at 3rd fret.

Verse

1. I thought I saw ___ a man brought ___ to life.

He was warm, ___ he came a - round ___ like he was

dig - ni - fied. He showed me what it was ___ to cry.

Verse

2. Well, you could-n't be ___ that man I ___ a - dored.
3. So I guess ___ the for - tune tell-er's right. ___

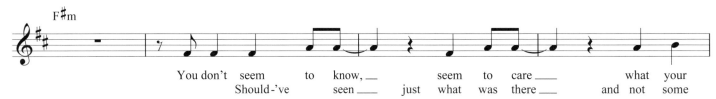

You don't seem to know, ___ seem to care ___ what your
Should -'ve seen ___ just what was there ___ and not some

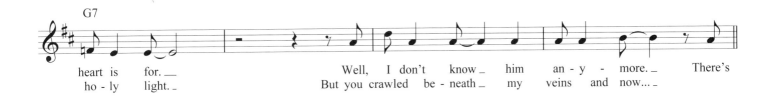

G7

heart is for. ___
ho - ly light. ___

Well, I don't know ___ him an - y - more. ___ There's
But you crawled be - neath ___ my veins and now... ___

Pre-Chorus

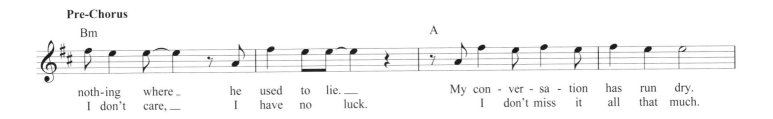

Bm   A

noth-ing where ___ he used to lie. ___ My con - ver - sa - tion has run dry.
I don't care, ___ I have no luck. I don't miss it all that much.

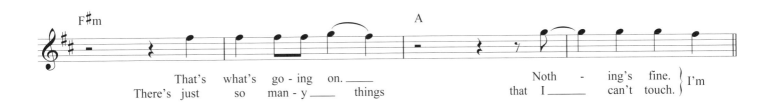

F#m   A

That's what's go - ing on. ___ Noth - ing's fine. } I'm
There's just so man - y ___ things that I ___ can't touch. } I'm

Chorus

D   A

torn.   I'm ___ all out of faith, ___ this ___ is how I

Bm   G

feel. ___ I'm cold and I ___ am shamed ly - ing na - ked on the

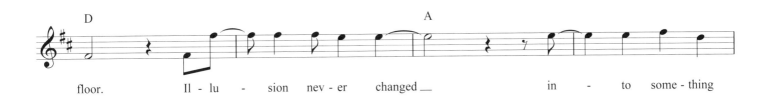

D   A

floor.   Il - lu - sion nev - er changed ___ in - to some - thing

Bm   G

real. ___ I'm wide a - wake ___ and I can see the per - fect sky is

torn.   You're a lit - tle late.   I'm

al - read - y torn.

Torn.

Interlude

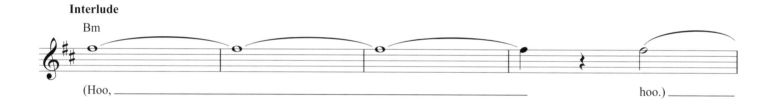

(Hoo,   hoo.)

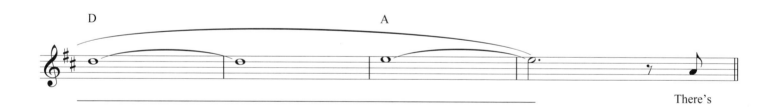

There's

Pre-Chorus

noth - ing where he used to lie.   My in - spi - ra - tion has run dry.

That's what's go - ing on.   Noth - ing's right. I'm

Treasure

Words and Music by Bruno Mars, Ari Levine, Philip Lawrence, Fredrick Brown and Thibaut Berland

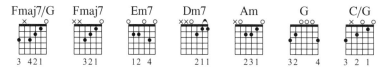

*Capo III

Strum Pattern: 5
Pick Pattern: 1

*Optional: To match recording, place capo at 3rd fret.

Intro
Moderately

Verse

1. Gim - me your, gim - me your, gim - me your at - ten - tion,
2. Pret - ty girl, pret - ty girl, pret - ty girl, you should be

ba - by: I got - ta tell you a lit - tle some - thing a - bout your -
smil - ing.   A girl like you should nev - er look so

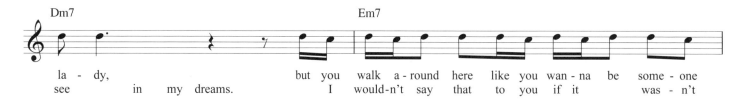

self.   You're won - der - ful, flaw - less, oo, you're a sex - y
blue.   You're ev - 'ry - thing I

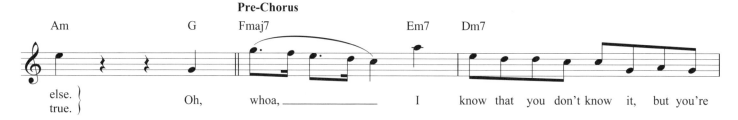

la - dy,   but you walk a - round here like you wan - na be some - one
see   in my dreams.   I would - n't say that to you if it was - n't

Pre-Chorus

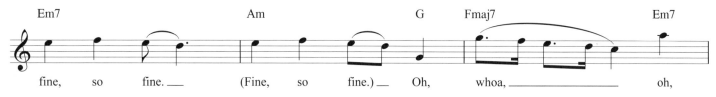

else. }   Oh, whoa, _____ I know that you don't know it, but you're
true. }

fine, so fine. ___ (Fine, so fine.) _ Oh, whoa, _____ oh,

girl, I'm gon-na show you, when you're mine, all mine. __ (Mine, all mine.) __

𝄋 Chorus

Trea-sure. That is what you are. Hon-ey, you're my gold-en

star. You know you can make my wish come true if you let me trea-sure

3rd time, To Coda ⊕

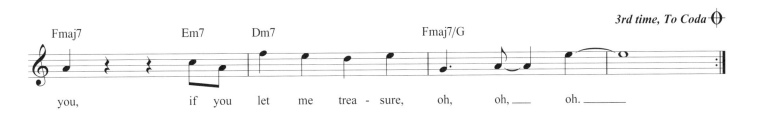

you, if you let me trea-sure, oh, oh, __ oh. _____

Bridge

You are my trea-sure, you are my trea-sure, you are my trea-sure, yeah,

you, you, you, you are. You are my trea-sure, you are my trea-sure,

⊕ **Coda**

D.S. al Coda **Outro**

you are my trea-sure, yeah, you, you, you, you are.

Repeat and fade

Trouble

Words and Music by Ray LaMontagne

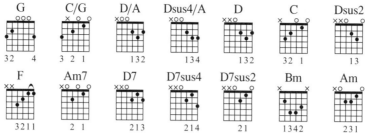

Strum Pattern: 9
Pick Pattern: 7

Intro
Fast

Verse

1. Trou - ble, _____
2. Trou - ble, ___

_____ trou - ble, trou - ble, trou - ble, trou - ble.
oh, _____ trou - ble, trou - ble, trou - ble, trou - ble.

Trou - ble been dog - gin' my soul since the day I was born, ___ ah.
Feels like ev - 'ry time I get back on my feet, she come a - round _____ and knock me down a -

Wor - ry, _____
gain. Wor - ry, _____ oh, ____

wor - ry, wor - ry, wor - ry, wor - ry. Wor - ry just
___ wor - ry, wor - ry, wor - ry, wor - ry. Some - times I

will not seem to leave my ___ mind _____ a - lone. ___
swear it feels like this wor - ry _____ is my on - ly friend.

Well, I've been

Chorus

a, saved _____ by _____ a wom - an.

I've been a, saved _____ by ____

_____ a wom - an. I've been a, saved _____

___ by _____ a wom - an. She won't

let me go, _____ she won't let me go, _____ now.

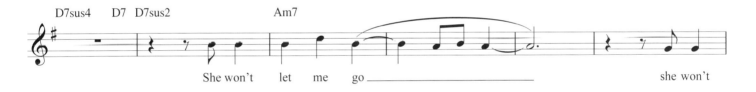

She won't let me go _____ she won't

1.
Interlude

let me go _____ now, now.

2.
Bridge

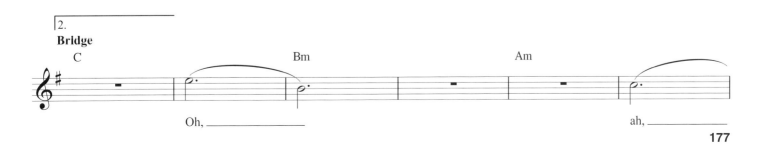

Oh, _____ ah, _____

177

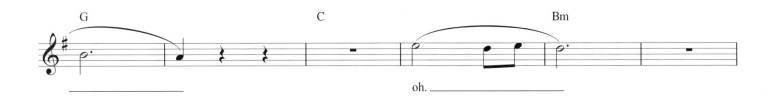

oh.

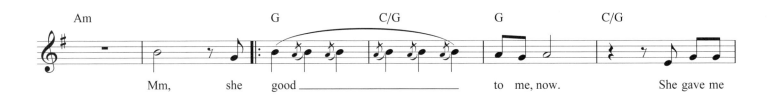

Mm, she good _____ to me, now. She gave me

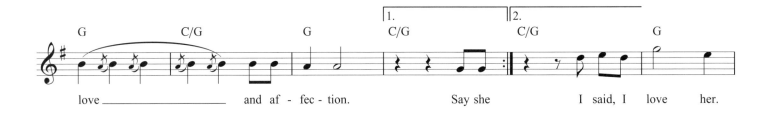

love _____ and af - fec - tion. Say she I said, I love her.

Yes, I love her. I said, I love her. I said, I love. _____

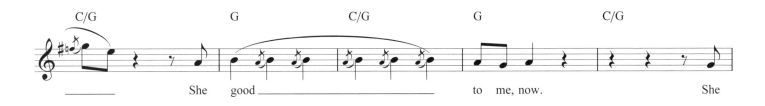

_____ She good _____ to me, now. She

Outro

good to me. She good to me. Mm. _____

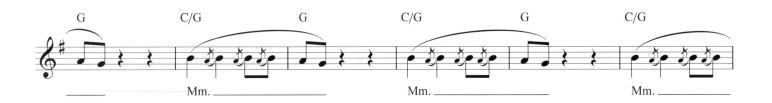

_____ Mm. _____ Mm. Mm.

The Way I Am

Words and Music by Ingrid Michaelson

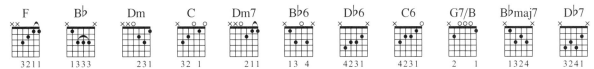

Strum Pattern: 6
Pick Pattern: 6

Try

Words and Music by busbee and Ben West

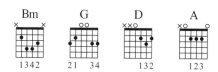

Strum Pattern: 1
Pick Pattern: 5

Intro
Moderately

1. Ev - er won-der 'bout what he's do-ing, how it all turned to lies?
2. Fun - ny how the heart can be de - ceiv-ing more than just a cou - ple times.
3. Ev - er wor - ry that it might be ru - ined? And does it make you wan - na cry?

3rd time, To Coda 1

Some-times I think that it's bet - ter to nev - er ask why.
Why do we fall in love so eas - y, e - ven when it's not right?
When you're out there do - ing what you're do - ing, are you just get - ting by?

Chorus

Where there is de - sire, there is gon - na be a flame. Where there is a

flame, some - one's bound to get burned. But just be - cause it burns does - n't mean you're gon - na

3rd time, To Coda 2

die; you got - ta get up ___ and try and try and try, got - ta get up ___

and try, and try, and try, _____ got - ta get up _____ and try, and try, and

2nd time, D.S. al Coda 1

try.

⊕ **Coda 1**

D.S.S. al Coda 2

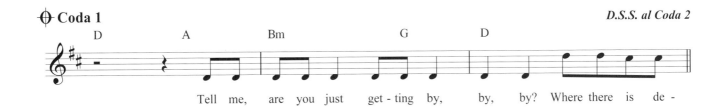
Tell me, are you just get - ting by, by, by? Where there is de -

⊕ **Coda 2**

and try, and try, try, _____ you got - ta get up _____ and try, and try, and

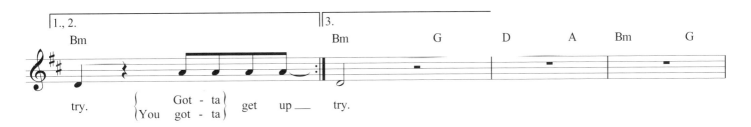
try. {Got - ta / You got - ta} get up _____ try.

Outro

You got - ta get up _____ and try, and try, and try, got - ta get up ___

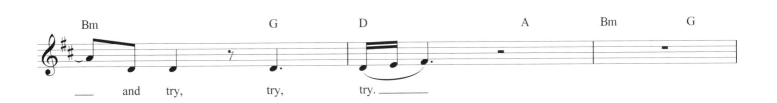
_____ and try, try, try. _____

Unwell

Words and Music by Rob Thomas

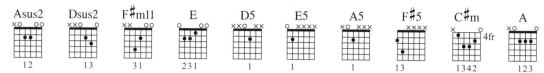

Strum Pattern: 3
Pick Pattern: 3

Intro
Moderately slow, in 2

Verse

1. All day, star-in' at ___ the ceil-ing mak-in' friends with
   be. 2. Me, talk-ing to ___ my-self in pub-lic and dodg-ing

shad-ows on ___ my wall. All night,
glanc-es on ___ the train. And I know, I

hear-in' voic - es tell-in' me ___ that I should get ___ some sleep be-cause ___ to -
know they've all ___ been talk-ing 'bout ___ me. I can hear ___ them whis-per and it

mor-row might be good for some - thin'. Hold on. Feel-in' like ___ I'm
makes me think there must be some - thing wrong with me. Out of all ___ the

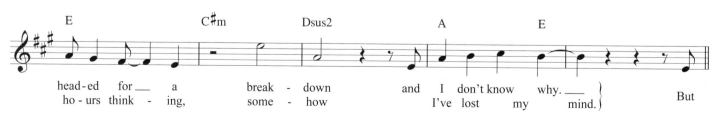

head-ed for ___ a break - down and I don't know why. ___ But
ho-urs think - ing, some - how I've lost my mind. ___

We Are Young

Words and Music by Jeff Bhasker, Andrew Dost, Jack Antonoff and Nate Ruess

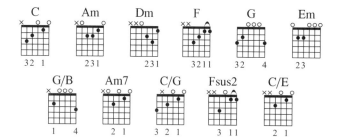

*Capo V

Strum Pattern: 1
Pick Pattern: 5

Verse
Moderately

1. Give me a sec-ond, I, I need to get___ my sto-ry straight. My

*Optional: To match recording, place capo at 5th fret.

friends are in the bath - room get-ting high - er than the Em - pire State. My

lov - er, she's wait-ing for me just a - cross___ the bar.___ My seat's been

tak - en by some sun-glass - es ask-ing 'bout a scar.___ And I know I gave it to you

months a - go;___ I know you're try - ing to for - get.___ But be -

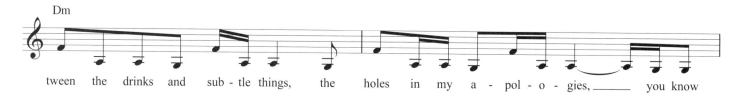

tween the drinks and sub - tle things, the holes in my a - pol - o - gies,___ you know

I'm try - ing hard to take __ it _____ back. So, if by the

Pre-Chorus
Slower

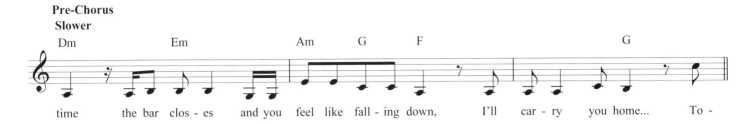

time the bar clos - es and you feel like fall - ing down, I'll car - ry you home... To -

𝄋 Chorus

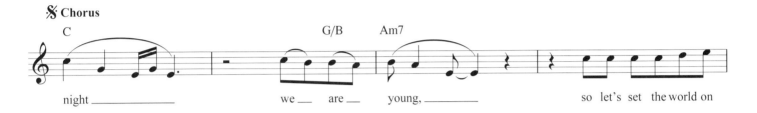

night _____ we __ are __ young, _____ so let's set the world on

fi - re; we can burn bright - er than the sun. _____

To - night _____ we __ are __

young, _____ so let's set the world on fi - re; we can burn

2nd time, To Coda 1 𝄌

3rd time, To Coda 2 𝄌

bright - er than the sun. _____ 2. Now I

Verse

know that I'm not _____ all that you've got. I guess that I, I just thought

Dm

may - be we could find new ways to fall a - part. But our friends are back,

D.S. al Coda 1

Fsus2   G

so let's raise a toast, _____ 'cause I found some-one to car - ry me home... _ To -

⊕ Coda 1   **Bridge**

G   C   F   C/E

_____   *Female:* Car - ry me home to - night. _   Just car - ry me home to - night. _

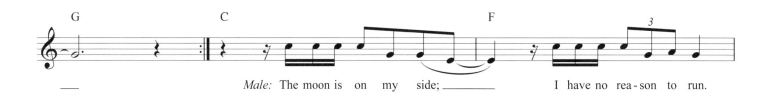

G   C   F   *3*

_   *Male:* The moon is on my side; _____ I have no rea - son to run.

C/E   G   C

So will some-one come and car - ry me home to - night? _____ The an - gels nev - er ar - rived, _____

D.S. al Coda 2

F   C/E   G

_ but I can hear the choir.   So will some-one come and car - ry me home... _ To -

⊕ Coda 2   **Outro**

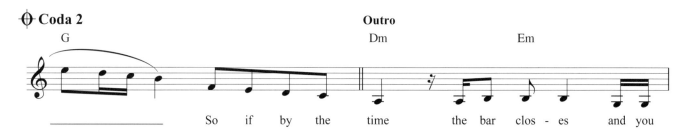

G   Dm   Em

_____   So if by the time the bar clos - es and you

Am   G   F   G   C

feel like fall - ing down, I'll car - ry you home ____ to - night.

What Makes You Beautiful

Words and Music by Savan Kotecha, Rami Yacoub and Carl Falk

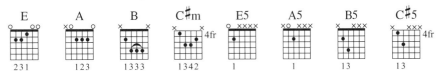

Strum Pattern: 3
Pick Pattern: 3

Intro
Moderately

1. You're in - se -

Verse

cure,   don't know what   for.   You're turn - in' heads when you walk through the
mon,   you got it   wrong.   To prove I'm right, I put it in a

do - o - or.   Don't need make - up   to cov - er up.   Be - ing the
so - o - ong.   I don't know why   you're be - ing shy   and turn a -

Pre-Chorus

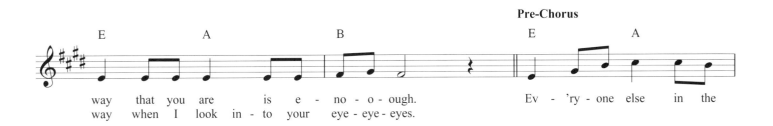

way that you are   is e - no - o - ough.   Ev - 'ry - one else in the
way when I look in - to your eye - eye - eyes.

room can see   it,   ev - 'ry - one else but   you,   oo.   Ba - by, you

% Chorus

light up my world like no - bod - y else. The way that you flip your hair gets me

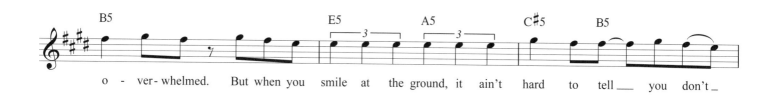

o - ver - whelmed. But when you smile at the ground, it ain't hard to tell __ you don't __

*Chords in parentheses played 3rd time.

know, oh, oh, you don't know you're beau - ti - ful. If on - ly you saw what

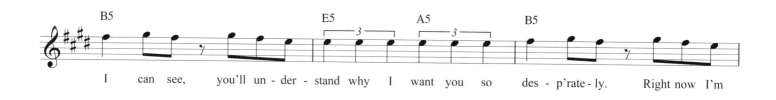

I can see, you'll un - der - stand why I want you so des - p'rate - ly. Right now I'm

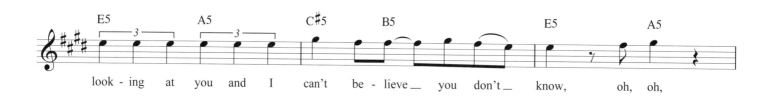

look - ing at you and I can't be - lieve __ you don't __ know, oh, oh,

3rd time, To Coda

you don't know you're beau - ti - ful. Oh, oh, oh, that's what makes you beau - ti - ful.

Interlude

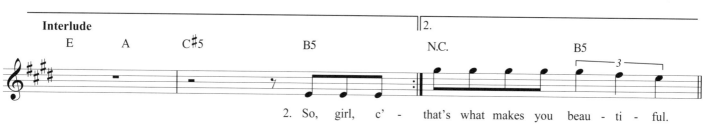

2. So, girl, c' - that's what makes you beau - ti - ful.

Bridge

Na, na, na, na, na, na, na, na, ___ na. Na, na, na, na, na, na.

Chorus

Ba - by you light up my world like no -

bod - y else. The way that you flip your hair gets me o - ver - whelmed. But when you

smile at the ground, it ain't hard to tell ___ (You don't ___ know, oh, oh...)

D.S. al Coda

Coda

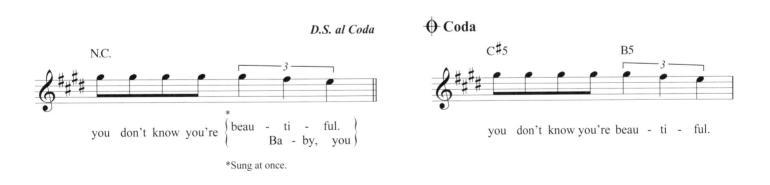

you don't know you're { beau - ti - ful. } { Ba - by, you }

*Sung at once.

you don't know you're beau - ti - ful.

Oh, oh, oh, that's what makes you beau - ti - ful. ___

What Hurts the Most

Words and Music by Steve Robson and Jeffrey Steele

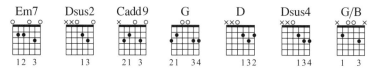

*Capo I

Strum Pattern: 3
Pick Pattern: 3

Intro
Slow, in 2

*Optional: To match recording, place capo at 1st fret.

Verse

1. I can take the rain on the roof of this emp-ty house, _
2. *See additional lyrics*

that don't both-er me. I can take a few tears now and then and just let 'em out. ___

I'm not a-fraid to cry, ev-'ry once in a while e-ven though go-in' on with you gone

still up-sets _ me. There are days ev-'ry now and a-gain I pre-tend I'm o-kay, but that's _

% Chorus

not what gets _ me. _____ What hurts the most {1., 3. was / 2. is} be-in'

so _____ close and hav-in' so much to say and watch-in' you

*Let chord ring.

**Let chords ring, next 4 meas.

Additional Lyrics

2. It's hard to deal with the pain of losin' you ev'rywhere I go,
But I'm doin' it.
It's hard to force that smile when I see our old friends and I'm alone.
Still harder
Gettin' up, gettin' dressed, livin' with this regret,
But I know if I could do it over,
I would trade, give away all the words that I saved in my heart,
That I left unspoken.

Who Will Save Your Soul

Words and Music by Jewel Murray

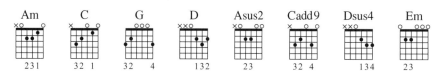

Strum Pattern: 6
Pick Pattern: 4

Intro
Moderately

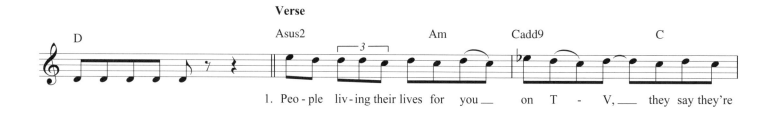

Verse

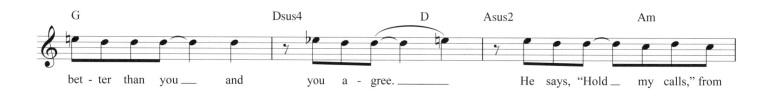

1. Peo - ple liv - ing their lives for you __ on T - V, __ they say they're

bet - ter than you __ and you a - gree. _____ He says, "Hold __ my calls," from

be - hind those cold __ brick walls. Says, "Come here, boy, there ain't __ noth - ing for free." __

An - oth - er doc - tor's bill, a law - yer's bill, an - oth - er cute, cheap thrill. You know you love him if you

Chorus

put him in your will. __ But who will save _____ your souls __ when it comes __

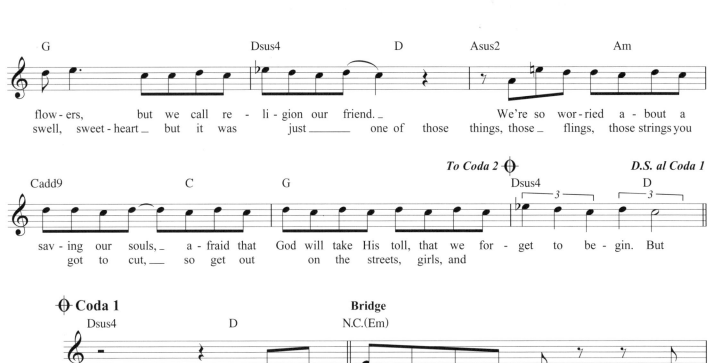

flow - ers, but we call re - li - gion our friend. _ We're so wor - ried a - bout a

swell, sweet - heart _ but it was just _ one of those things, those _ flings, those strings you

To Coda 2 ⊕   *D.S. al Coda 1*

sav - ing our souls, _ a - fraid that God will take His toll, that we for - get to be - gin. But

got to cut, _ so get out on the streets, girls, and

⊕ **Coda 1**   **Bridge**

D.S.S. al Coda 2

⊕ **Coda 2**   **Outro**

bust your butts."   Who will save _

_ your _ soul? _

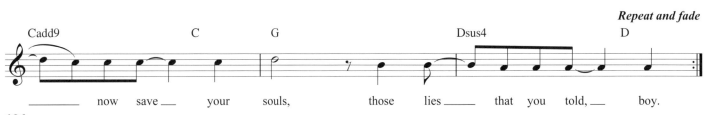

Ba - by, come _ lit - tle ba - by, yeah. Ha, ya, _ ha, ya,

Repeat and fade

_ now save _ your souls, those lies _ that you told, _ boy.

Wide Awake

Words and Music by Katy Perry, Lukasz Gottwald, Max Martin, Henry Walter and Bonnie McKee

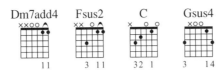

*Capo V

Strum Pattern: 1
Pick Pattern: 5

Intro
Moderately slow, in 2

(I'm wide a - wake.)   (I'm wide a -

*Optional: To match recording, place capo at 5th fret.

Verse

wake.)   1. Yeah, I was   in the dark. _   I was fall - ing hard _ with an
wake.)   2. Not los - ing an - y sleep. _   I picked up ev - 'ry piece _ and land - ed

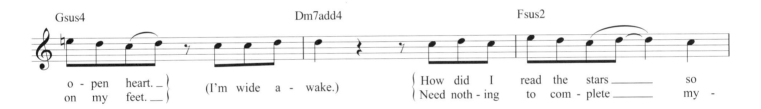

o - pen heart. _   (I'm wide a - wake.)   How did I read the stars ____ so
on my feet. _   Need noth - ing to com - plete ____ my -

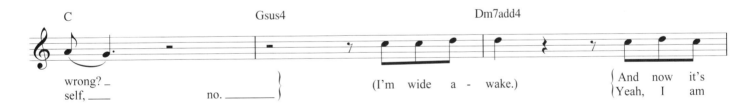

wrong? _   no.   (I'm wide a - wake.)   And now it's
self, ____   Yeah, I am

clear to me ____ that ev - 'ry - thing you see ____ ain't al - ways what it seems. _ (I'm wide a -
born a - gain ____ out of the li - on's den; ____ I don't have to pre - tend. _ (And it's too

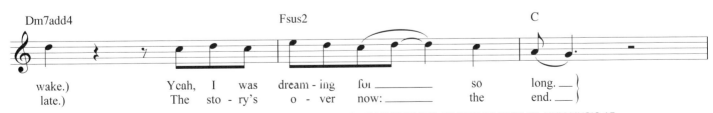

wake.)   Yeah, I was dream - ing for ____ so long. _
late.)   The sto - ry's o - ver now: ____ the end. _

Pre-Chorus

I wish I knew then what I know now; would-n't dive

in, would-n't bow down. Grav-i-ty hurts; you made it so

sweet un-til I woke up on, on the con-crete.

𝄋 Chorus

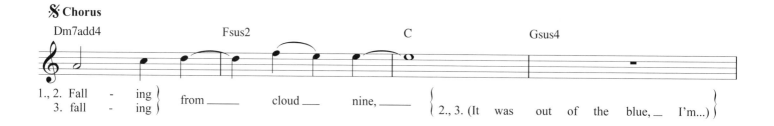

1., 2. Fall - ing } from ___ cloud ___ nine, ___ { 2., 3. (It was out of the blue, ___ I'm...) }
3. fall - ing }

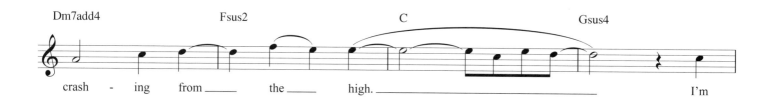

crash - ing from ___ the ___ high. ___ I'm

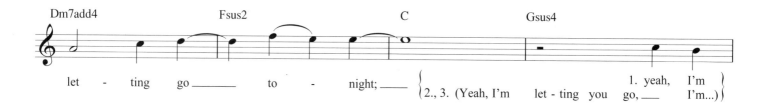

let - ting go ___ to - night; ___ { 2., 3. (Yeah, I'm let - ting you go, ___ I'm...) }

3rd time, To Coda ⊕

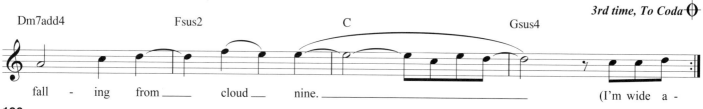

fall - ing from ___ cloud ___ nine. ___ (I'm wide a -

Bridge

wake.) Thun - der rum - bl - ing, . cas - tles

crum - bl - ing. I _____ am try'ng to _____ hold

on. _____ (I'm wide a - wake.) God _____ knows

that I _____ tried see - ing the bright _ side,

but I'm _____ not blind an - y - more. _____

Interlude

(I'm wide a - wake.)

D.S. al Coda

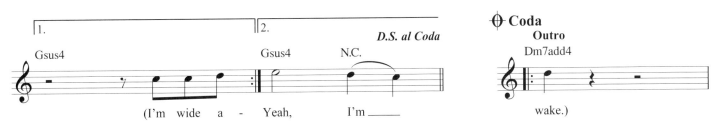

(I'm wide a - Yeah, I'm _____   wake.)

(I'm wide a - wake.)

Yellow

Words and Music by Guy Berryman, Jon Buckland, Will Champion and Chris Martin

Tuning:
(low to high) E-A-D-G-B-Eb

Strum Pattern: 1
Pick Pattern: 5

You and I

Words and Music by Jeff Tweedy

You're Beautiful

Words and Music by James Blunt, Sacha Skarbek and Amanda Ghost

You Belong with Me

Words and Music by Taylor Swift and Liz Rose

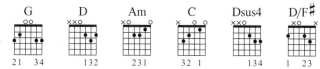

*Tune down 1/2 step:
(low to high) Eb-Ab-Db-Gb-Bb-Eb

Strum Pattern: 1
Pick Pattern: 5

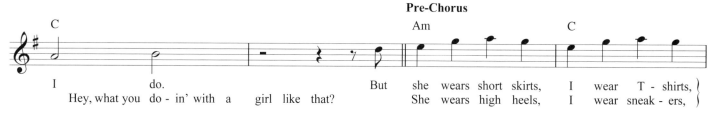

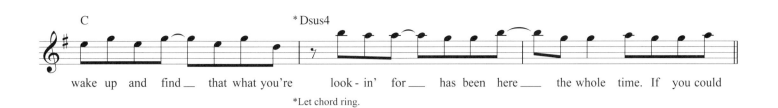

C   *Dsus4

wake up and find __ that what you're look - in' for __ has been here __ the whole time. If you could

*Let chord ring.

Chorus

G   D

see that I'm __ the one __ who un - derstands you. Been here all __ a - long, __ so why can't you

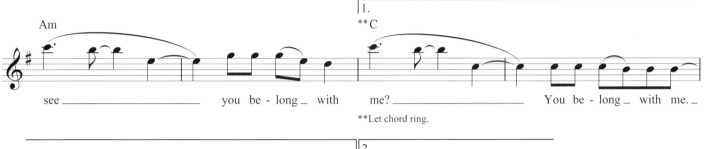

1.

Am   **C

see _____ you be - long __ with me? _____ You be - long __ with me. __

**Let chord ring.

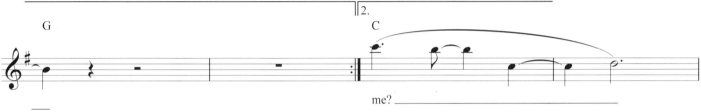

2.

G   C

__   me? _____

G   D

Stand - ing by __ and wait - ing at your back door. All this time __ how could __ you not know, ba -

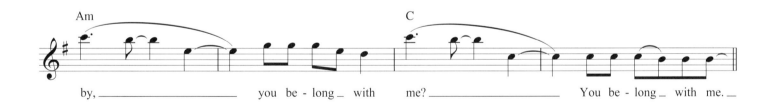

Am   C

by, _____ you be - long __ with me? _____ You be - long __ with me. __

Interlude

G   Dsus4   Am

__

Bridge

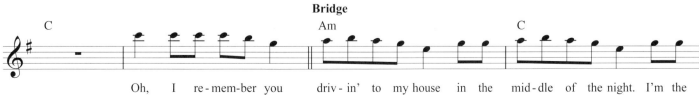

C   Am   C

Oh, I re - mem - ber you driv - in' to my house in the mid - dle of the night. I'm the

Guitar Chord Songbooks

Each 6" x 9" book includes complete lyrics, chord symbols, and guitar chord diagrams.

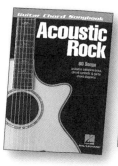  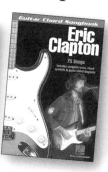 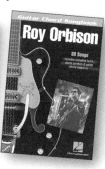 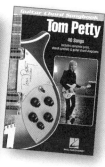 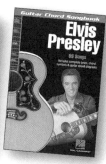 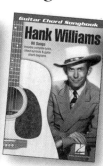

Acoustic Hits
00701787 . . . . $14.99

Acoustic Rock
00699540 . . . . $17.95

Adele
00102761 . . . . $14.99

Alabama
00699914 . . . . $14.95

The Beach Boys
00699566 . . . . $14.95

The Beatles (A-I)
00699558 . . . . $17.99

The Beatles (J-Y)
00699562 . . . . $17.99

Bluegrass
00702585 . . . . $14.99

Blues
00699733 . . . . $12.95

Broadway
00699920 . . . . $14.99

Johnny Cash
00699648 . . . . $17.99

Steven Curtis Chapman
00700702 . . . . $17.99

Children's Songs
00699539 . . . . $16.99

Christmas Carols
00699536 . . . . $12.99

Christmas Songs – 2nd Edition
00119911 . . . . $14.99

Eric Clapton
00699567 . . . . $15.99

Classic Rock
00699598 . . . . $15.99

Coffeehouse Hits
00703318 . . . . $14.99

Country
00699534 . . . . $14.99

Country Favorites
00700609 . . . . $14.99

Country Standards
00700608 . . . . $12.95

Cowboy Songs
00699636 . . . . $12.95

Creedence Clearwater Revival
00701786 . . . . $12.99

Crosby, Stills & Nash
00701609 . . . . $12.99

John Denver
02501697 . . . . $14.99

Neil Diamond
00700606 . . . . $14.99

Disney
00701071 . . . . $14.99

The Best of Bob Dylan
14037617 . . . . $17.99

Eagles
00122917 . . . . $16.99

Early Rock
00699916 . . . . $14.99

Folksongs
00699541 . . . . $12.95

Folk Pop Rock
00699651 . . . . $14.95

40 Easy Strumming Songs
00115972 . . . . $14.99

Four Chord Songs
00701611 . . . . $12.99

Glee
00702501 . . . . $14.99

Gospel Hymns
00700463 . . . . $14.99

Grand Ole Opry®
00699885 . . . . $16.95

Green Day
00103074 . . . . $12.99

Guitar Chord Songbook White Pages
00702609 . . . . $29.99

Hillsong United
00700222 . . . . $12.95

Irish Songs
00701044 . . . . $14.99

Billy Joel
00699632 . . . . $15.99

Elton John
00699732 . . . . $15.99

Latin Songs
00700973 . . . . $14.99

Love Songs
00701043 . . . . $14.99

Bob Marley
00701704 . . . . $12.99

Bruno Mars
00125332 . . . . $12.99

Paul McCartney
00385035 . . . . $16.95

Steve Miller
00701146 . . . . $12.99

Modern Worship
00701801 . . . . $16.99

Motown
00699734 . . . . $16.95

The 1950s
00699922 . . . . $14.99

The 1980s
00700551 . . . . $16.99

Nirvana
00699762 . . . . $16.99

Roy Orbison
00699752 . . . . $12.95

Peter, Paul & Mary
00103013 . . . . $12.99

Tom Petty
00699883 . . . . $15.99

Pop/Rock
00699538 . . . . $14.95

Praise & Worship
00699634 . . . . $14.99

Elvis Presley
00699633 . . . . $14.95

Queen
00702395 . . . . $12.99

Red Hot Chili Peppers
00699710 . . . . $16.95

Rock Ballads
00701034 . . . . $14.99

Rock 'n' Roll
00699535 . . . . $14.95

Bob Seger
00701147 . . . . $12.99

Carly Simon
00121011 . . . . $14.99

Sting
00699921 . . . . $14.99

Taylor Swift
00701799 . . . . $15.99

Three Chord Acoustic Songs
00123860 . . . . $14.99

Three Chord Songs
00699720 . . . . $12.95

Today's Hits
00120983 . . . . $14.99

Top 100 Hymns Guitar Songbook
75718017 . . . . $14.99

Two-Chord Songs
00119236 . . . . $14.99

Ultimate-Guitar
00702617 . . . . $24.99

Wedding Songs
00701005 . . . . $14.99

Hank Williams
00700607 . . . . $14.99

Stevie Wonder
00120862 . . . . $14.99

Neil Young–Decade
00700464 . . . . $14.99

Prices, contents, and availability subject to change without notice.

HAL•LEONARD® CORPORATION
7777 W. BLUEMOUND RD. P.O. BOX 13819 MILWAUKEE, WI 53213

Visit Hal Leonard online at **www.halleonard.com**

0514

HAL LEONARD GUITAR CHEAT SHEETS

The Hal Leonard Cheat Sheets series includes lyrics, chord frames, and "rhythm tab" (cut-to-the-chase notation) to make playing easier than ever! No music reading is required, and all the songs are presented on two-page spreads to avoid page turns.

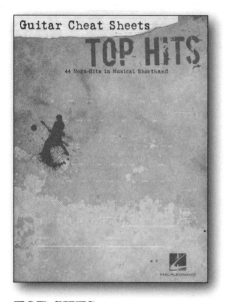

TOP HITS

44 pop favorites, including: Are You Gonna Be My Girl • Baby • Bad Day • Bubbly • Clocks • Crazy • Fireflies • Gives You Hell • Hey, Soul Sister • How to Save a Life • I Gotta Feeling Just the Way You Are • Lucky • Mercy • Mr. Brightside • Need You Now • Take Me Out • Toes • Use Somebody • Viva La Vida • You Belong with Me • and more.
00701646 ....$14.99

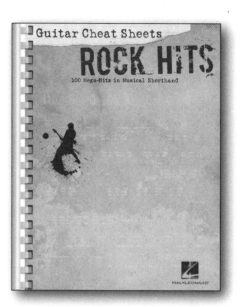

ROCK HITS

44 songs, including: Are You Gonna Go My Way • Black Hole Sun • Counting Blue Cars • Float On • Friday I'm in Love • Gives You Hell • Grenade • Jeremy • Kryptonite • Push • Scar Tissue • Semi-Charmed Life • Smells like Teen Spirit • Smooth • Thnks Fr Th Mmrs • Two Princes • Use Somebody • Viva La Vida • Where Is the Love • You Oughta Know • and more.
00702392 ....$24.99

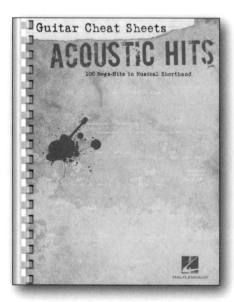

ACOUSTIC HITS

100 unplugged megahits in musical shorthand: All Apologies • Crazy Little Thing Called Love • Creep • Daughter • Every Rose Has Its Thorn • Hallelujah • I'm Yours • The Lazy Song • Little Lion Man • Love Story • More Than Words • Patience • Strong Enough • 21 Guns • Wanted Dead or Alive • Wonderwall • and more.
00702391 ....$24.99

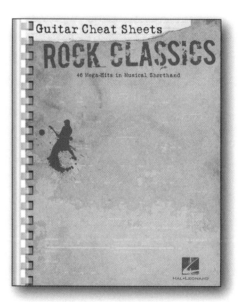

ROCK CLASSICS

Nearly 50 classics, including: All Right Now • Barracuda • Born to Be Wild • Carry on Wayward Son • Cat Scratch Fever • Free Ride • Layla • Message in a Bottle • Paranoid • Proud Mary • Rhiannon • Rock and Roll All Nite • Slow Ride • Smoke on the Water • Sweet Home Alabama • Welcome to the Jungle • You Shook Me All Night Long • and more.
00702393 ....$24.99

HAL•LEONARD®
CORPORATION
7777 W. BLUEMOUND RD. P.O. BOX 13819 MILWAUKEE, WI 53213

Visit Hal Leonard online at www.halleonard.com   *Prices, contents, and availability subject to change without notice.*   0712